D1322220

Federico Ezequiel Gargiulo

Fire
Walking

Tales of an expedition to the End of the Earth

SÜD
POL

Fire

To Leo and Juan,
my expedition partners and friends.

To my parents.

To all those who venture
into remote lands.

Gargiulo, Federico Ezequiel
    Fire walking : tales of an expedition to the end of the earth / Federico Ezequiel
Gargiulo ; ilustrado por Nahuel Mieres. - 1a ed. 1a reimp. - Ushuaia : Südpol, 2009.
    208 p. : il. ; 23x15 cm.

    Traducido por: Ignacio Valencia Rú
    ISBN 978-987-24524-0-7

    1. Relatos de Viaje. I. Mieres, Nahuel, ilus. II. Valencia Rú, Ignacio, trad. III. Título
    CDD 910.4

©2008. Federico Gargiulo
©2008. Editorial Südpol
(9410) Ushuaia - Tierra del Fuego - República Argentina
www.sudpol.com

Diseño de tapa e interior: Magali Canale | Pica y punto
info@picaypunto.com.ar

Ilustraciones de interior: Nahuel Mieres
nahuel_mieres@hotmail.com

Versión en inglés: Ignacio Valencia Rú - Cecilia Della Croce
Corrección general: Don Taylor

Todas las fotografías son propiedad del autor
excepto las señaladas.

Impreso en Argentina - *Printed in Argentina*

Primera edición: agosto de 2008
Segunda edición: noviembre de 2009

ISBN: 978-987-24524-0-7

Hecho el depósito que marca la ley 11.723
Libro de edición argentina

Index

Prologue

The task of introducing the reader to the unknown universe of an unpublished story, narrated by an unknown author, in just a few lines, is not an easy one. Nevertheless, I must admit that I feel honored for having been chosen to introduce the forthcoming pages by means of this preface, with these simple words, which one way or another, shall serve as the host to a book where there is no waste.

Reading the pages of *Fire Walking* over and over again made me - for I carry it in my blood - recall my great-grandfather, expert Francisco Pascacio Moreno, who actively took part in the research, development and exploration of the wildest, remotest and most solitary regions of Patagonia. In fact, come to think of it, since it was my good fortune to be one of the first to plunge into this young man's adventures, I can easily see the connection between the plans, goals and ideals of these two adventurers. Although this connection straddles two centuries of different social, political and economic contexts and a country that has changed its configuration in all senses, its very essence and its truest self have remained unchanged.

Like the hero of days gone by – Francisco Pascacio Moreno - the author shows a special love for Patagonia; a love that sometimes can only be understood by those of us who share the same feeling. Just like Perito - as our family likes to think of him - Gargiulo expresses himself, in his descriptions, ideas and experiences, in a clear and simple way, and weaves in, with the freshness of his style, a fair amount of history. He does so by means of the most sincere method available to universal writing: speaking from the heart. Lastly, to conclude that connection that I just briefly outlined, I might add that both Moreno and the writer have undergone great perils and misfortunes, with the aim of exploring, discovering and, ultimately, sharing.

Turning away from reminiscences, and before letting you enjoy this new literary work, I have the moral obligation to make a few recommendations to you, reader: Set your imagination free, take a mental journey along the lines and depths of this narration, enjoy the sweet moments, laugh out loud with the happy ones and weep with the bitter ones; let your spirit fly towards those dream places, feel the sand under your feet and the cold wind biting your face; experience the icy waters hitting your chest with each river crossing, enjoy the dancing lights cast by the bonfires defying the Southern nights. There is not much left to say, just wish you good luck in this walk of over five hundred kilometres, in this pilgrimage that will make you travel through everlasting dream landscapes filled with history, which started on a day just like any other, in the same way my great-grandfather ventured, over two centuries ago, into far-away lands.

Adela Benítez Moreno
(Great-granddaughter of expert Francisco Pascacio Moreno.)

Introduction

This book does not claim to be a source of consultation of the most significant aspects of the history of Tierra del Fuego. Here you will find the adventures of three men who, in the course of walking over five hundred kilometres, courageously brought to bear the necessary strength and energy to surmount a hostile environment, a land of mystery, solitude and isolation.

The reader will not find here the testimonies that are usually written under the faint lamp of a dark library, but the feelings, emotions and experiences of three adventurers, those that are born deep inside a forest, on a distant and deserted beach, or at the top of a perfect mountain. In the following pages, you will explore the legends, myths and the story of a place that has halted in time, of a place where the spirits of sailors, conquistadors, martyrs and eccentrics still wander about looking for fortunes.

This work does not intend to represent every cultural detail of this remote place, but to hint at them by virtue of real contacts, through the magic felt seeing every wreck, hearing about every exile and every event, right where they once took place, by feeling the wind blowing in our faces, the water running through our fingers, the sand tickling our feet, and the fire lighting our nights.

These lines are nothing but the chronicle of an adventure loaded with emotions, joy, tears and sadness, feats and failures, victories and defeats. Do not look for scientific, botanical or historical terms in these pages. If you decide to go ahead and read this book, you will find the honest words that stem from the heat of souls and hearts, from imagining stories right where they were actually born.

F. E. G.

Note to the English edition

Often, those things related to the habits and folklore of a certain people bring about problems when trying to convey their meaning in other languages. Situations such as reading this book, sometimes call for small solutions that pave the way to a better understanding by the reader. That is why for this English edition I have decided to shed some light on certain terms - related to regionalisms and typical Argentinean traditions - to which I will constantly refer throughout this text, and that will be a common place in my story. Moreover, in the notes below, I have added some information about the trees that the reader will find mentioned in the pages of this adventure. Those of you interested in this work will benefit greatly by understanding these terms, and will get a fuller and richer experience from this tale; the story of three young men and a journey through the most remote and desolate places of Tierra del Fuego.

F. E. G.

Mate

Mate is an infusion prepared by steeping dried, chopped and ground leaves of yerba mate (Ilex paraguariensis) - a South American plant - in hot water. The name derives from the quechua term mati, which means glass or drinking vessel. It became widely used for referring to the calabash gourd (Lagenaria siceraria) used for that infusion. Its high caffeine (also called mateine) content makes this drink, like tea, coffee or chocolate, a strong stimulant.

As the act of drinking *mate*, matear, entails the intake of a great deal of water, it also serves as a purifying infusion, and through its antioxidant elements it protects the body. *Mate* is somewhat acid, so other herbs – to aid digestion, regulate the hepatic function, produce a sedative effect, etc - are sometimes added in small proportions. These herbs neutralize acidity as well offset the powerful stimulating effect of caffeine.

Traditionally, it is drunk hot by means of a metal straw – that also acts as a sieve - directly from the gourd. It can be drunk bitter or sweet.

Everybody, from the humble to the rich, has the habit of drinking *mate*.

Even in the way it is prepared - a ritual in itself - *mate* is characterized by its uniqueness.

Unlike tea or coffee, served in individual cups, *mate* represents a whole different process when it comes to brewing it (cebar).

There is a long list of rules and traditions that apply to brewing and enjoying *mate*, too long to be fully included is this introduction. Among the most relevant:

The infusion is served around a circle during the 'mateada', a gathering for drinking *mate*.

The pourer, usually the host, drinks up the first *mate*, until air is drawn from the metal straw.

Then the pourer subsequently refills the gourd and passes it to the next drinker in the circle – with the straw in his direction - who likewise drinks it all, without thanking the pourer.

The ritual proceeds around the circle in this fashion until the *mate* becomes *lavado* (washed out or flat).

The fact that the straw is shared makes the mate-drinking experience a unique one, and specially intimate, so intimate that some people compare drinking *mate* to kissing.

For that reason, *mate* is not shared with just anybody, quite the opposite. You share that experience with people you care about, because in sharing *mate*, you share your soul, and you do that just with relatives, close friends or your significant other. Without a doubt, *mate* is more than a drink; it is an element of union, a symbol of trust, friendship and intimacy among those who share it.

Tortas fritas

These are the traditional accompaniment to a proper *mateada*. In Argentina, *tortas fritas* are part of rural tradition. Generally, when rain makes it impossible to work in the open air, it is customary for the woman of the house to prepare them. They are made with flour, water, salt and fat; the dough is kneaded until a soft consistency is achieved, it is flattened out and informally cut into pieces. A small hole is made in each of them. They are finally fried in beef, pork or mutton fat. *Tortas fritas* go with *mate* in endless rounds, where anecdotes and stories are told for the pleasure of the gathered friends.

Dulce de leche

Dulce de leche (Milk jam): is a typical Argentinean food product. It is the result of slowly cooking milk and sugar with a dash of vanilla.

Lenga (*Nothofagus pumilio* – High deciduous beech) is a deciduous tree native to the southern area of the Andes range. It can reach up to 30 metres high (96 feet). In Tierra del Fuego it grows up to the timberline, at about 600 – 650 metres above sea level. In the autumn their dark green leaves turn to yellow and reddish tones. Many houses in Tierra del Fuego are built with its wood, because of its good quality. It is also used in furniture. Most of the Fuegian forest comprises *lenga*.

Guindo (*Nothofagus betuloides* - Evergreen beech) is an evergreen tree, which grows up to 25 metres (82 feet). Found from sea level to 500 metres (1600 feet).
The wood has beautiful marks, is pinkish, hard and semi-heavy. Long pieces of the bark of this tree were used by natives to build the canoes they used to sail through the Beagle Channel.

Ñire (*Nothofagus antarctica* – Low deciduous beech) is a deciduous tree native to southern Chile and Argentina. It´s the smallest deciduous beech tree in Tierra del Fuego: it grows between 10 and 15 metres high (30-48 feet).
The leaf color is similar to that of *lengas,* and turning yellow and orange in autumn. The hard wood of this tree was often used by rural workers to build fences.

Canelo (*Drimys winteri* - Winter's bark) is an evergreen tree, which grows up to 20 metres (65 feet) tall. It normally grows alongside the *guindo*, and is found mainly along the Beagle Channel Coast.
The bark is gray, thick and soft and can be used as a pepper replacement. *D. winteri* was an important source of vitamin C for the seafarers of the 18th century, because it helped to heal the scurvy, a very common disease of these days.
The wood, red and heavy, was used by natives to build harpoons, which were used to hunt sea lions.

'Although one day

the Columbuses, Magellans, Cooks, Franklyns, Livingstones, who discovered new worlds and who died in the process of showing them to us, will not find even modest imitators because of the lack of setting and because the terrestial sphere (which is both great and small) will be familiar even in its furthest reaches, those who follow the steps of Galileo, Voltaire, Humbolt and the like will never cease to exist.

They will complete the knowledge of the world; everything that exists will be revealed by their studies, and there will be a day when the human spirit will reign over everything that was ever created or uncreated. The world will then be Man's worthy pedestal.'

Francisco Pascacio Moreno

1
Gestation

In the course of his voyage, Magellan saw many lights
shining night and day on the lands that extended to the South
of the channel, and called that region the Land of Fire.

ALBERTO M. DE AGOSTINI

Back in 1998, as a way of celebrating my graduation from high
school, I decided to go on holidays with two friends of mine:
Ruy and 'Fat' Robert. I remember that trip because it was the
first time I slung a backpack over my shoulder and headed off
to explore Patagonia from Bariloche to Esquel... hitchhiking,
by bus, for two weeks. That was also the first time I set foot on
the other side of the Colorado River, which marks the beginning of Patagonia.

Although the details of the trip itself are not relevant, I must
speak about something that happened inside of me. I deeply
believe that life is filled with symbols, instants, periods that
leave their mark on you in a unique way, that imprint your fate
onto your heart.

I suddenly met Patagonia face to face. I entered the 'Land
of Giants'. I guess that my destiny was defined right there, in
that very moment, forever. I started loving nature and its
unmistakable breath, the woods, lakes and mountains, those
stone sculptures that constantly amaze me, even to this day.

Unfortunately, I was still too young to explore the area and
I had to start college, but I was not willing to resign myself to
forgetting about the wonders of Patagonia. Perhaps I could not
travel physically, but nothing could prevent me from travelling

with my mind. I bought a book, 'Viaje a la Patagonia Austral' (Travel to Southern Patagonia), written by expert Francisco Pascacio Moreno. Reading its passages was like flying across bright blue skies, surpassing snow-capped mountain peaks, feeling the harsh winds on my face and falling more and more in love with that feeling of tranquility and solitude that invades my soul and skin every time I say the word Patagonia.

If I had to name my idols, no doubt Perito - as I like to call him affectionately - would be one of them. Without him, the map of Argentina would now have a different shape. There would be other borders and boundaries. Were it not for his explorations, reports and protest letters, today Patagonia would share with us a different story - not that the centralist rulers of Buenos Aires would have cared...

From Moreno I moved on to Musters, Cox and Piedrabuena, another staunch champion of Argentine sovereignty. Of course, as is frequently the case in this life of ours (or at least in this country), those who take a stand and fight tooth and nail to defend a just cause, as Moreno and Piedrabuena did, die impoverished, and are condemned to oblivion. They are only remembered on their centennial, when some small group takes a commemorative plaque to a deserted island on a navy boat and performs a gun salute, to later on forget that we stand where we stand because of them.

I lived in Buenos Aires for four years, but the life I led in that metropolis did not make me happy. Right after graduating, I set my mind on Patagonia. I ended up in Ushuaia, the 'end of the world', which was my initiation to Magellan's 'Land of Smoke', the land of Onas, Yamanas, Alakaluf and Haush.

I knew quite a bit about Patagonian history, but little about that Island to the south of the Magellan Strait. It was with great enthusiasm that I read about seafarers that set course for the Southern Atlantic. I learned that Dutch, Spanish and even English people had observed those lands during their journeys aboard their wooden ships, propelled by cathedral-like sails, which shook as the hulls were being pounded by gigantic waves.

I became increasingly familiar with names such as Shouten, Le Maire, Nodal, Elizalde, De Agostini and Fitz-Roy. Filled with curiosity I examined every bay, cove and whatever geographical feature I could find on the Island of Tierra del Fuego.

Despite its vastness, there was only one part that I felt especially attracted to: the Mitre Peninsula, that piece of land to the east of the Island, surrounded by the cold waters of the Atlantic and separated from Staten Island by the feared strait of Le Maire.

I would spend long hours contemplating maps, where I could see the exact location of hundreds of shipwrecks around the peninsula, marked by the drawing of a little vessel with its name underneath. My mind would wander over tales of shipwrecked sailors, adventurers, corsairs and daring explorers. Tales of ambition, secret orders, European empires and mutinies on the high sea invaded my head every time I observed the fascinating cartographic wonders of Tierra del Fuego.

It was then that I started making enquiries about the existence of trails or paths to get there, and I must admit that the answers I got were far from encouraging. Every bit of information pointed at the fact that very few people, hardly anyone really, ventured into those faraway lands. Maybe it was for that precise reason that, over the following three years of my life, I became obsessed with the peninsula. I imagined myself walking on those desolate places, naturally virgin and wild, where the only sounds were the whirring wind and the roaring waves. I had developed a deep romanticism for that spot which stuck in my mind.

Months became years, one after the other like pages in a book, and during all that time I gained trekking and camping experience. The natural environment and the dreamlike landscapes of Isla Grande of Tierra del Fuego little by little engulfed me. I would still spend long hours contemplating the map of the Island, but no longer as a romantic or a dreamer, but as an astute observer, an analyst weighing real possibilities. Getting there would not be an easy task; I knew it would require great physical strength, and a fair amount of mental preparation.

On a day like any other in October 2004, I was coming down from Cerro del Medio, a hill near the city of Ushuaia with a friend of mine, Juan Manuel Ronco. We were both watching the city from high up above and, as it sometimes happens in life, we made the inexplicable decision to plan to travel on foot to the southeastern end of the Island. Yes, that peninsula for which we shared so many feelings, which attracted us so compellingly and for no clear reason. We agreed on a departure date, which would be the first day of May of the following year. After all that time of imagining and dreaming, the possibility of solving the mystery of those remote places first hand became a reality. We decided to invite someone else, a sort of 'third musketeer.' Some days later, Juan told me he had already found the third and last member of our imminent expedition: Leonardo Fernández, someone whom I had never met before.

2
Preparations

*...only in Tierra del Fuego have I felt the deep feelings
that are awakened in the traveller's soul by nature's great feats..*

RAMÓN LISTA

The idea then turned into a reality; our adventure towards the
Mitre Peninsula was already an event that would soon take place. We had only six months left to plan down to the very last
detail of the expedition.

At the beginning, we considered various possibilities and
schedules full of uncertainties. But later on, and thanks to
references provided by previous visitors to those lands[1], we
were able to determine our itinerary more accurately. The
three of us decided upon the route for our adventure: our
goal was to start in Ushuaia and get to Estancia María Luisa,
walking along the coast of the Beagle Channel and the icy
Atlantic Ocean. We calculated that it would take us somewhere between 35 to 40 days to cover such great distance.
None of us had taken part in an adventure of the sort, which
turned planning into a complicated task. We spent hours, days
and even a few sleepless nights pondering over the various

---

1. During the months that preceded the expedition, we gathered information from those who
had already been there. People like Sergio Anselmino, Beto Brizuela and Adolfo Imbert helped
us greatly by sharing with us their personal experiences in the Mitre Peninsula in detail.

alternatives, trying to find the best options in terms of gear, food and clothing.

The Argentinean Navy offered to take two boxes filled with provisions up to Buen Suceso outpost for us, onboard the ship *Alférez Sobral*. That generous cooperation by the Navy made it possible for us to carry less weight on our backs, since a big part of our supplies for the adventure would travel aboard that ship; the rest, we would carry ourselves.

Things were pretty much organized, but we lacked an emblem, something that would identify us as a team, as an expedition. The three of us agreed on 'Nomads in Mitre' as a name. We would never settle for long, just like the Yamanas moved for thousand of years, we would slowly keep going over the changing terrain, like nomads.

We did not want to turn the whole field experience into mere personal glory. So, we decided to add another mission to the adventure. In this way, we turned 'Nomads in Mitre' into a more ambitious project that would encompass an educational side. Why keep all those rich experiences to ourselves? Why hide the information about the place, if we could actually share it with other people? The three of us decided that youth would be the most appropriate addressee for the information we could provide after our return.

On this second stage of the project we would devote ourselves to passing on information about the geography, flora and fauna of the peninsula at every educational institution in Ushuaia, sharing our personal experience from the expedition. Our intention was to raise awareness about the environment among the young and bring them closer to nature and outdoors activities, induce them to respect nature and in that way, try to offer an alternative to the dangers and uncertainties that they are usually exposed to in their urban lives.

We made our project official, and obtained the support and sponsorship of private companies and governmental institutions. They made it possible for us to get more and better gear, and to procure all the supplies that our expedition required.

The last few days just before departure were critical. It seemed that our very own, self-constructed Tower of Babel would come tumbling down over unsteady and muddy soil. I felt nervous and anxious, filled with expectations and, at times, fear. But there was no turning back; the cards had been dealt and it was our time to play.

3
TheAdventureStarts

From Ushuaia to Moat

*The journey of a thousand miles
begins with a single step.*

LAO TSE

DAY 1 Not everyone took our journey as something positive. Many, even several colleagues of ours, tried to talk us out of it. 'Crazy', 'insane' and 'delirious' were some of the adjectives they used to refer to us. They could not understand how we could even think about walking in the most absolute solitude, for hundreds of kilometres, for over thirty days. We knew that May was not the best time of the year to set off, but it was the only time the three of us could do it. From the very beginning, we knew that days would be cold and short, but we had taken those facts into consideration when planning our project. It could be said that we were counting on not bumping into any surprises; we planned for the worst from the outset.

Finally, on May 1st 2005, the three of us embarked on a journey that we had planned for six months. The place that saw our expedition start was Escarpados beacon, at the end of provincial road 30, just a few kilometres out of Ushuaia.

We were happy; we took pictures and made our debut in the seventh art: besides our photographic gear we carried a camcorder to keep a more accurate record of our findings.

We started walking slowly following the trail to Estancia Túnel[1]. The day was gorgeous, the sun shone across the cloud-free sky. Our backpacks were very heavy, about 35 kg each. The trail there is very clearly marked and has the typical gentle hills carved by a glaciation[2]. This area is rich in *lenga* trees (high deciduous beech, *Nothofagus pumilio*), although *ñires* (low deciduous beech, *Nothofagus antarctica*), *notros* (fire bush, *Embothrium coccineum*) and *canelos* (winter's bark, *Drimys winteri*) can be found.

It took us about an hour to get to the estancia. We did not stop there, as the three of us already knew the place. The site is where the first sawmill became operational on the coast of the Beagle Channel[3]; it gained prestige for its wooden casks (*toneles,* in Spanish), casks that eventually changed the name of this rural establishment. The reason is in words and phonetics: the Spanish word 'tonel' is similar both in its written and oral form, to the current name of the Estancia: Túnel (tunnel). I do not know exactly when or why the name changed from *tonel* to *túnel.* Behind an abandoned *rancho* (hut), we could see rusty machinery, a big wheel and a steam boiler, ancient witnesses to the sawmill's faded splendor. I should also mention that the oldest native Yamana settlements were found right here. They are over 6,500 years old and various elements of the Yamana culture were found there, like scrapers and

---

1. An Estancia is the Spanish word for ranch. These ranches are usually larger than ranches in North America and England.

2. The whole Island of Tierra del Fuego is believed to have been covered by glaciers during the Pleistocene (between 100,000 and 20,000 years ago.) Ice expanded over each glaciation, while the withdrawal process occurred during the Interglacial periods, Holocene, which usually leave marks of their activity. That is how the glacial valleys were formed and the glacial and hanged valleys, with their 'U' shape, as well as the glacial cirques. The Beagle Channel was formed by a gigantic ice river, probably 1,200 metres high.

3. The Beagle Channel was originally called 'Onachaga' by the Yamanas, meaning 'the channel of the Onas.' The current name coincides with the name of the ship of its discoverer, Robert Fitz-Roy. He was an essential part of the biggest mapping exercise in the history of Tierra del Fuego and the Patagonian coasts, commissioned by the British Crown between 1826 and 1836. That exercise named many islands and features of the Fuegian archipelago, such as Navarino, Picton and Lennox, Murray channel, Woodcock and Snipe Islets, etc.

arrow and harpoon heads, which have shed some light on the evolution of this ethnic group.

We left the estancia behind and an hour later we got to the banks of Encajonado River. It actually looks like a stream, if compared to the rivers we would be wading across some days later. This was the only time we took our boots, socks and trousers off before crossing. And let me tell you why. Since for the rest of the journey, we spent all day walking on humid and muddy terrain, riddled with peat bogs[4] where we would sink in, sometimes up to our knees, we thought that taking our clothes off before crossing a river was pointless, as we were already soaking wet.

Perhaps you can understand what I felt upon touching the icy water if I told you that it was like being stung on the legs by a thousand bees at the same time.

At noon, we stopped to grab a bite. We ate cheese, ham and crackers. Unluckily, we did not have much time to spare - we had to get on the move shortly after, as our bodies started to cool down.

It took us almost three hours to get to Estancia Punta Segunda. We found no one there, although some hints made us think that someone did indeed live there: dogs, a four-wheeler in excellent condition and some horses. We left our things inside a big wooden shed and we set ourselves to lighting a fire. It took us a while, but we succeeded. I was the first one to delight the group with my cooking skills: we savored some noodles with cheese soup. The after-dinner conversation took place over some *mate,* as we reflected and discussed the most relevant aspects of the day. We spoke about what the journey that we had just started that morning meant for us.

---

4. Peat bogs are old lagoons formed by the retreat of glaciers, whose beds were filled with clay. These in turn were filled, in whole or in part, by organic and, to a lesser extent, inorganic deposits. Due to the high acidity, the constant saturation of water and low temperatures, there is little bacterial activity, so dead moss never decays fully, and builds up on the bottom and sides of the lagoon. With the passing of time, the lagoon gets filled up. Over 90% of a peat bog is thought to be water.

The three of us knew that it would be long, but we were confident that we could accomplish it. I had known Juan for quiet a while and I had met Leo when we started preparing for the expedition. But it was only then that we started to really know each other, no masks or shields to hide our inner selves. We all had a great interest in the Mitre Peninsula. We wanted to know every inch and every story. But we never imagined that during that trip we would get to know more than just a beautiful landscape. That adventure would also be an introspective journey and would reveal, almost imperceptibly, all those things that we ignored about ourselves.

We went to bed around midnight, under a starry sky.

DAY 2 The sleeping bags did a great job. I managed to get the much-needed rest, as I was never cold. We got up at seven thirty, not to the singing of birds but to the artificial and monotonous beeping of my alarm clock.

I boiled some water and we had a blend of granola, dried fruits, chocolate and powder milk for breakfast; we decided to call that blend the 'product mix'.

The morning was chilly and we could clearly see some frosted water pools. Luckily, Phoebus gave us a hand and shone bright, warming the air a bit.

The landscape between Punta Segunda and Estancia Remolinos is perhaps one of the most beautiful ones that I have ever seen. Vast extensions of green grass, gentle hills and the waters of the channel, a plain and simple landscape, without great features, just the necessary ones to render it unforgettable. We were in good spirits, so we moved fast and determinedly. But at the same time, the place was so amazing that we felt the need to stop and take pictures and just bask in the beauty of nature. Before reaching the main house at the estancia, we drank some *mate* and ate some salami, although this time we indulged ourselves in some chocolate for dessert.

We followed a kind of natural highway, unknowingly created by the tame cows that grazed in those grasslands. There they were, hundreds of them, quite likely upset by the unexpected and unwelcome invasion of three colourful beings.

The Estancia Remolinos (which means 'eddies') is very significant in the history of Tierra del Fuego, as it belonged to one of the pioneers who got to the end of the world: John Lawrence. This man settled in Ushuaia with his wife, Clara Lawrence, in 1873. The couple was one of the first white settlers to live on the island. Thomas Bridges[5] asked them both to be part of the

---

5. Thomas Bridges (1842-1898) was an Anglican missionary and sheep rancher in Tierra del Fuego. He was born in Lenton, Nottingham, England in 1842. He was adopted by the Rev. George P. Despard, Pastor of Lenton, and came with the Despards to Keppel Island in the Falkland Islands (Islas Malvinas) in 1856 at the age of 13. He learned the native Yaghan or Yamana language, and in September 1871 settled on Tierra del Fuego with his wife Mary Varder and infant daughter Mary (1870-1922) at what is now the city of Ushuaia. I will refer to him in the following pages.

Anglican Mission. Before settling in Ushuaia, the Lawrence's devoted themselves to preaching at a Mission station in the Malvinas islands (a.k.a. the Falklands) region, at an islet called Keppel. Once in Ushuaia, John Lawrence started teaching. After twenty-five years of non-stop work at the Mission, President Roca granted Lawrence the use and exploitation rights for Estancia Remolinos, in recognition of this humanitarian effort. That same year, on January 30th, his wife passed away and that fine man decided to move to the estancia till the day he died, at age 89. The sustained decline of the aboriginal people made him think that there was not much of a future for the mission.

The shipwrecked *Monte Sarmiento* lies, motionless, in front of this estancia. In 1911, while loading cargo and passengers, this vessel hit a rock. Luckily, the captain reacted, manoeuvrering in the most logical way, taking the ship as close to the coast as possible, and running it permanently aground. Thank God there were no casualties.

The estancia is nowadays property of the Argentinean Navy and is used by its members to perform training manoeuvres.

There is a road that goes all the way up from this place to Almanza port. A project is underway to link it to provincial road 30 (the one that leads to Escarpados beacon, the starting point of our expedition.) I have no doubt that initiatives like this are clearly against the survival of landscapes around the world.

We started seeing some houses to the sides of the road, as we were reaching Almanza port. As of late, lots of people have settled there to develop micro-businesses, such as mussel harvesting and king crab fishing. Not very long ago, power lines were run in order to assist human habitation.

On the opposite bank of the channel, we could already see Puerto Williams, the military base on Navarino Island. The population, of about two thousand, is directly related to the Force, although there are a few civilians that make a living out of fishing.

I must admit that my shoulders hurt a lot; I felt a constant pressure that weakened me both physically and mentally. My friends also carried excessive weight on their backs, especially

Leo, who carried the biggest pack. It was already night time, and we still had eight kilometres to go to reach Almanza port. Unfortunately, we knew that the whole way there would be uphill.

Just before walking the last kilometres, climbing the hill that would take us to the much-expected refuge, a man with a truck offered to take us to the port on the next day. That night we camped next to his house, not very far away from where we were. I do not remember his face, or his name, but I do remember his last words to us: 'Don't you dare throw a single piece of paper, I'm old and grumpy!' Of course we did not, and we were not planning to. It is good for the world to have people like that who care about every piece of land being clean, wherever that piece of land might be.

We put up the tent for the first time, placing the gear under the apse[6] to protect it from the soft but constant drizzle that had pervaded the night. Once inside the sleeping bags and under canvas, we had soup for dinner. We talked and record- ed our notes on video for a while. We each told the camera, as if it was an invisible journalist, what we had done during the day. The three of us agreed on something: we were carrying too much weight; on the next day, we would leave food and other unnecessary things at Almanza port.

---

6. The apse is an extension of the tent that has a roof, but it does not have a floor. It can be used to store backpacks, to cook or put away things that will not be needed during the night.

DAY 3 We had accepted the generous offer made by the man we met the previous night, which implied getting up at five in the morning, because he came to pick us up at seven sharp - he had warned us about his punctuality; anyway, I believe that no living organism in that area could sleep through the roaring of his truck's engine.

We jumped on the back part and we were on our way. Those last eight kilometres to Almanza were very exposed and cold. Had we walked the previous night (it was all uphill), I am sure that we would have grumbled about it, especially taking into account how tired we were before setting up the camp.

Twenty minutes later, we reached our destination. We had already decided that we were going to leave some weight over there. We had two alternatives: the Navy or the Coast Guard outpost. We decided in favour of the Coast Guard. We had already made the decision, now we only had to knock on the door and unexpectedly wake up the people who lived there. A man promptly invited us to step inside, with no signs of being annoyed, although he looked a little bit surprised. We explained the reasons of our visit and Juan Franco, our host, invited us to have some *mate* with him. When he brought the tray full of *tortas fritas*, we exchanged a conspiratorial look with Juan, for we had mentioned during our walk that *tortas fritas* were a must when in an outpost.

Before leaving, we opened our packs and started to leave enormous amounts of food, foreseeing that we would find more at every outpost we visited. I left my fishing rod, and a box of hooks and sinkers, a book (*On Heroes and Tombs* by Ernesto Sábato) and a knife that weighed about one kilogram, something Leo and Juan made fun of.

After that episode, I learned that you only need to carry that which is absolutely necessary: every additional element turns into unnecessary weight and, in the long run, becomes a pain.

We put the extra gear and food in a box. We gave it to Juan Franco and got ready for departure. We would pick it up upon arriving in Ushuaia. We thanked him and another guy who had arrived a while before and then we left.

That day we needed to walk about twenty kilometres to get to Estancia Harberton along the inner road J. That time it was a delight to lift the packs. They were much lighter and more comfortable. After unloading, we felt like we were flying.

Walking along a road can be disheartening, but if you take it easy, it can even turn into a relaxing experience. I think that this part of the trip was like a prologue to what would come next. During this section, which is by no means short (about one hundred kilometres), we got used to carrying weight for long hours, although there were no obstacles or difficulties to overcome. We just had to move forward like robots towards the finish line.

After five hours and a half, we got to Estancia Harberton. I must put the story on hold now for a while, to tell you that this was the first estancia on the Island of Tierra del Fuego, founded at the turn of the 19th century by Thomas Bridges, an English Anglican missionary. In recognition of his evangelizing labor with the Yamanas, Julio Argentino Roca, the then president of Argentina, gave him 20,000 hectares, including mountains, lakes and bays outlooking the Beagle Channel. The area developed into an important sheep raising region, although now it is only used for tourism[7].

The scenery is absolutely beautiful. Green hills, several houses and sheds along the same aesthetic and building line: tin structures painted white on the outside, red roofs, green doors and window frames.

The estancia is currently inhabited by the English missionary's great-grandson, Thomas Goodall, and his wife, an American biologist called Natalie Rae Procer. I found 'Tommy', whom I had met before, and after telling him about our plan to walk tirelessly all the way to the peninsula, he offered the shearing hut for us to spend the night under shelter.

A little later, we shared some *mate* with Leo and Juan while we watched the colours of the day give way to the inks of the night. Briefly afterwards Juan Carlos, the foreman of the estancia, came to kindly invite us to have some *mate* with him

---

7. Estancia Harberton was declared a National Historic Monument by Decree 64 in 1999.

and his wife inside the house. It was impossible to turn such a pleasant offer down. It felt so nice to be in there! It was comforting to listen to the cracking of logs inside the salamander stove. That special sound made the whole situation feel very welcoming. As a whole, it was undeniable that the room had created a special atmosphere in which each object and person seemed to belong, an atmosphere where everything was friendly.

Then Ramona, Juan Carlos' wife and head of the kitchen, entered the room. We all felt at ease and we told them our story. They told us their life story and how they had ended up there, after many occupations related to the rural life. They were both very nice people and had a very special sense of humor.

Ramona surprised us bringing pizzas and pasta with meat. Leo, Juan and I ate heartily, not only because we were hungry, but because everything was delicious. We contributed with some chocolate for dessert.

It was in that place where we started to get to know, first hand, the values of the people who live in the countryside. By far, they are not the wealthiest people - I am not referring to landowners here - but they are so generous that they will give you everything they can. They do not care about nationality, age or political affiliation; they are honest and humble people who are always trying to help others, something that is hardly seen in city folks. Their way of living, their habits and generosity are truly admirable. I wish I could find people like that more often.

That night, Juan Carlos gave us something that would be of utmost importance in our expedition: a kind of wick to light fires. He told us that he made them himself by leaving pieces of porous wood under burnt oil for a few days. They facilitated the task of whoever had to light the fire.

Before going to bed, Juan read some fragments of Martín Fierro, the book that he had chosen as entertainment by the firelight.

DAY 4   We took some pictures of the shearing hut under the golden morning light. We said goodbye to Juan Carlos and Ramona and that was the beginning of a new day for us. We started walking along the edge of the Cambaceres inner bay. In the area, Thomas Bridges' children devoted a lot of time to raising cattle with the help of several young Yamana men. Leaving history aside for a moment, and speaking more subjectively, I confess that I found that landscape to be plainly beautiful.

The night had covered the soil with frost, rendering it firm and allowing us to walk faster. The most important aspect of the day was that we went beyond the limits of Estancia Harberton and entered Estancia Moat, which is currently owned by the Lawrence family. None of us had been there before, which meant that we were entering a new and unknown world.

From there onwards, vegetation starts to change quite radically. There are hardly any *ñires* or *lengas*, and most of the forest is made up by *guindos* and *canelos*. Because of its great tree density and thickness, it resembles a rainforest. According to Rodolfo Iturriaspe, this can be explained in the following way[8]:

> '*In the Mitre Peninsula area, the mountain range consists of low altitude hills, and does not constitute the orographic barrier that can be found on the western part of Tierra del Fuego. This special feature, added to the lack of orographic obstacles in Hoste and Navarino Islands, create an environment that is more exposed to the winds coming from the southwest and hence to more oceanic conditions than those that can be found on the lands facing the Beagle Channel, between Harberton and Ushuaia, i.e. higher relative humidity values and probably rainfall.. This is evidenced in the vast development of peat bogs and the presence of flora that is uncommon further to the west... Rainfall is distributed throughout the year*

---

8. ITURRIASPE, Rodolfo, in *Península Mitre – Proyecto de creación de un área protegida en el extremo sudoriental de la Isla Grande de Tierra del Fuego, República Argentina*, page 11.

*without a dry season, caused by the movement of fronts that origi-
nate at polar latitudes of the South Pacific Ocean.'*

We continued along road J and from there we could see, on
the opposite bank of the Beagle Channel, the Picton, Lennox
and Nueva Islands. In 1980, there was a conflict over these
islands between Argentina and Chile. The conflict was related
to national boundaries. There were several high level discus-
sions to determine the destiny of these 'three rocky outcrops',
as a wise Argentinean president called them. Finally, a conclusion was reached: the three islands would be part of the
Chilean Republic for good. Although the relationship
between both countries got very tense at times, there it didn't
come to an armed conflict.

On that afternoon, we said goodbye to a great friend of
ours: Navarino Island. We could no longer see that familiar
outline that had accompanied us from the beginning of the
journey.

We camped near a small river. The site was gorgeous, located right in front of a Chilean islet called Snipe, where there is
an outpost that carries the same name. A vessel called *Logos* hit
the islet early in the morning of January 5th, 1988. The ship
from Singapore was special, because it was a library-ship.
Before the wreck, it used to sail the world as a Christian mission. Its crew, from all nationalities, disembarked at various
ports to spread the word of the Lord, organizing courses and
conferences. Other members of the crew stayed on board the
ship to sell the books. In some nations, like Muslim countries,
where non-official religions are somewhat limited, the *Logos*
initiative used to be the only chance that people had to pur-
chase Christian books.

The impact damaged the hull and the boat keeled over, so
there was no choice left but to evacuate immediately to the
nearest town, Puerto Williams. Argentinean and Chilean vessels helped with the evacuation. Luckily, almost 140 people
were rescued with no panic, although the ship itself was completely lost and passengers and crew could not even recover

their personal belongings. The ship can still be clearly seen, emerging from the icy depths of the ocean, as if wanting to start sailing the seven seas once again.

I fell asleep a little before Leo and Juan; they kept on reading Martín Fierro by the firelight.

DAY 5   That morning we were as precise as a Swiss watch. We got up really early and, without wasting any time, we had breakfast, packed away and left immediately. It was nine o'clock. It was one of the few times that we kept to that early schedule. As days went by, we headed out increasingly late. But not out of laziness, but because each day was shorter than the previous one, as autumn gave way to winter. Dawn took longer and longer to rise every week, and it was a very hard challenge for us to leave our tent in the dark, and face a wet, freezing full day.

Anyway, the team started to march over kilometres of deserted roads. Over these last few days Leo's foot started to ache, and Juan felt a pain on one of his heels. At first, I got worried. I was afraid that those pains would get worse over time and that, somehow, they could hinder our progress. Later on, I analyzed the facts and came to the conclusion that it was perfectly normal to feel muscle aches, since we walked with a lot of weight for long distances - about twenty five kilometres a day. Besides, the pace was quite brisk.

We stopped by the side of the road to have some lunch. Leo and Juan took pictures of a red falcon, while I rested my legs. Late that afternoon, we got to Estancia Moat, which was founded in 1902 by Antonio Isorna, a Spaniard who got to Ushuaia on an expedition commanded by Augusto Laserre in 1884[9].

---

9. The 'División Expedicionaria al Atlántico Sud', an expedition organized by the National Navy, reached the bay of Ushuaia on Sunday, September 28th, 1884. It was under the command of Navy Colonel Augusto Laserre. This initiative was a token of the government's willingness to create, in Tierra del Fuego, a sea navy outpost as a way to show sovereignty in those southern seas and lands. Before arriving to the coasts of the Island, Laserre visited Staten Island in April and established in its eastern end, on the bay currently known as 'San Juan del Salvamento', a navy outpost and a lighthouse. It is worth mentioning that there is a long established debate on the date of its foundation. Some people say October 12th, 1884 is when Ushuaia was founded, as that day Augusto Laserre created the navy outpost and the Argentine flag was hoisted for the first time in that region. Nevertheless, other people say that it was just the opening of an outpost of the Navy, while Ushuaia's true foundation day is the Decree dated June 27th, 1885, issued by the National Government by request of the governor of the Territory, Félix M. Paz, which established the political division of the new government with Ushuaia declared as the regional capital city, in the same place where Laserre had established the Navy outpost.

His descendants still live in Ushuaia and, currently, as I already mentioned, the estancia belongs to the Lawrence family. There were no signs of people there. And we did not stop to check, because our goal was to get to the Coast Guard outpost, which we could already see at a distance. To cheer Leo and Juan up, I told them that we were only five hundred metres away, but we actually had to walk about three kilometres to get there, as the road made some turns to cross the Moat River by means of a bridge. That innocent phrase 'five hundred metres' would become one of the many phrases that we repeated over and over again during the expedition. After that, each time one of us asked how much longer for a given place, the natural answer that jokingly came from the other two members was: 'five hundred metres!'

As soon as I crossed the bridge, I heard the unmistakable singing of woodpeckers[10]. I immediately heard the impact of their beaks on the tree trunks and, when I looked towards the source of the pleasant sound, two giant woodpecker (*campephilus magellanicus*) couples came in sight. Their size truly answers to the adjective in their name. This species that inhabits Tierra del Fuego is the biggest in size compared to other woodpeckers in South America. I told Leo and Juan, who were only fifty metres behind me, and the three of us just stood there, silent, enjoying that unique percussion show. These birds are really beautiful, specially the males, with their entirely red heads. Females are a little bit smaller and their head is black, with a kind of downward-looking ringlet.

Before reaching the outpost, we stopped at a house of Estancia Puerto Rancho. We were received by a man called Cárdenas. He gave some tips to take into account when crossing the rivers that were coming up ahead, as we continued our eastbound route. He asked us if we were carrying 'something strong for the throat.' 'What?' I asked, puzzled. He repeated the question and then I got it. He wanted alcohol. 'No, we don't have any,' we told him. A couple of months later, in

---

10. Its chant resembles laughter, and is used for drawing the attention of the opposite sex.

Ushuaia, I learned that Cárdenas had died of cirrhosis. It was sad to know that the farmer had fallen under the grip of alcohol.

We finally reached outpost Moat, property of the Argentinean Coast Guard. At first, we were not received as we had imagined, and for a moment I thought that they would tell us: 'There's plenty of room to camp over there, kids. If you need hot water, just holler.' Luckily, we broke the ice and felt at ease quite quickly, and they invited us to sleep over there. We had some *mate*, but no *tortas fritas* this time, although the stew that they fed us for dinner made up for that transgression against tradition.

I do not know if it was something spontaneous or an expression of desire or the answer to some sort of prayer, because, soon after entering the house, they asked if we felt like having a shower. No doubt they wanted us to plunge into the bathroom not for our sake, but for theirs.

Once again, we were treated like royalty. We had a pleasant conversation, watched TV and played 'Ten Thousands', a dice game were you have to be 'daring', as I said to my new friends and my team members. I did not win this time, just like in any other competitions that I took part in during my life.

We radioed a 'no news' to Leo's wife (in Ushuaia), via Mackinlay and Almanza outposts. This would be the last place where we would find people until we reached Buen Suceso Bay, on the eastern end of the Island. Perhaps, we might get lucky and find a lost soul along the way, but that was unlikely. It was better not to give it much thought; we had to move forward and focus on the road, for despite having already walked quite a bit, our adventure was just beginning.

4
OfftheBeatenTrack
From Moat to the Plastic Rancho

López River?... I don't know it.
And I don't want to know it.

CÁRDENAS *(local farmer)*

DAY 6 For the last few days, we had been thinking about our first walk 'off the beaten track', as we referred to the part of the journey after Moat. I felt like a soldier who trains for years, with effort and conviction, to go out to the battle fields one day, to face the harsh reality of war. Like those soldiers, I had mixed feelings, triggered by the novelty of it all, by the challenge posed by that which is unknown. My soul was filled with fear, anxiety, but mainly, hope. Because, after all, there is some sense in the saying that goes 'hope is the last to die'. I am certain that we would not have made it without hope lighting our hearts.

After having some *mate*, we thanked the people from the outpost and left with the first bright sun rays. During the day we crossed our second river, and this time we had to wait for the low tide. The river was fast flowing but not much water ran in it, so we did not have a hard time crossing it.

Given the specific route that we followed, mainly along the coast, our relationship with the sea and its tides was of the essence. Every six hours the water level went up or down, so we absolutely had to anticipate those movements accurately. We got the information from a tide cycle chart that we got from the Argentinean Navy. Logically, the tide cycle affected the water level of every river. During high tide rivers grew and in low tide they carried less water.

The trail had vanished; only at times was there a faint track to be found. We would have been better off following the coastline all day. I say this because later that day we wanted to take a shortcut and we ended up on a peat bog. The soil was very wet and unstable, and this made us fall a couple of times or got us wet with freezing water more than knee deep. Quite honestly, I was the one who had the most incidents in that sense, and the guys made fun of me for that. Of course I did not get mad; you had to take things lightheartedly in order to keep the morale high. That team spirit made us move forward at ease, not feeling burdened, even under the most adverse conditions.

Now that I give it more thought, like a historian drawing conclusions about ancient periods of history, I realize that our capacity to laugh at our own flaws was one of our best weapons to accomplish our mission.

Cárdenas had told us that upon crossing the river we would find two *ranchos*[1]. We made a brief stop at the first one, where we had some *mate* and tuna. The place was inviting enough for a stop, especially on such a nice day. Although it was cold, the sky was clear and the sun shone bright, almost defiantly

We were determined to sleep under a nice roof that night, so we resumed our walk to find the second *rancho*, which according to the *gaucho* was supposedly located three hours ahead. We sped up and avoided unnecessary stops. It was already five in the afternoon and it was starting to get dark, and we still saw no sign of the much hoped for refuge. We decided to keep going for another hour, and if there was no sign of the *rancho* yet, we would put up the tent. Just before minute sixty, with almost all hope lost and when we were about

---

1. The word 'rancho' is actually another way of saying outpost. Outposts are small structures (mostly tin and wood) used by farmers or laborers to rest during the night. Inside, it is common to find beds, dry firewood and sometimes even food. In this area, the main activity is the 'bagualeo', the herding of wild animals.

to set up the tent, Juan saw a wire fence. He walked ahead a bit, and from a hill he extended his arms and shouted: '*Rancho*!' The three of us started to shout like crazy, cheering and chanting, like pirates who, after sailing for many years, miraculously had found the treasure of the Spanish Armada. That cry of victory became our trademark; from that moment onward, each time one of us caught a glimpse of one of these wooden structures, we would let the cry out, strong and powerful, until it could be heard up in the clouds of heaven and down in the fiery pits of hell.

The small refuge was buried deep in a very picturesque spot. From there, the east coast seemed endless. The *rancho* was a wood and tin structure far from being a palace, but it seemed like one to us. That night we would sleep in that very basic shack, which meant we would not have to set up the tent, and we could light a fire under a roof and dry our clothes.

I was the first one to go in. The guys stayed out for a while, taking pictures of the perfect sunset. When I came out, eating some *charqui*, Juan gave me a puzzled look, not understanding what I was chewing. I explained to him that it was dried and salted meat; the food that the *gauchos* used to take with them on their riding trips, for it could last for years without going bad.

I had always wanted to try it. I never imagined that it could be so tasty. It tastes like Parma ham. Leo and Juan also liked it.

It was a relief to shelter from the cold winds and feel the warm embrace of the fire. We ate supper and then had our usual literary moment. As it was customary for us when reading from *Martín Fierro*, we had some *mate*. José Hernandez has written many long and beautiful passages about the rural life of times of yonder, passages that blend old customs with the everyday life of gauchos. And coming back to the Argentinean infusion, Leo and Juan were the ones to take the lead on that matter. I was always less of a 'traditionalist' and more of a 'gringo'. I usually drank tea, and if lucky enough to find it, coffee. Anyhow, it was always very nice to share in a round of *mate*. I guess it is because this infusion has something that the others do not: the virtue of generating a feeling of union, friendship and comradeship.

As Leo and Juan read the adventures of gaucho Fierro, I could not help but think about those men of days gone by, travelling the empty pampas, over endless miles of Argentinean land. I imagined them and their ponchos, their horses and their knives. Many of them had to live in small forts, exposed to the fearsome *malones* or raids that used to afflict border towns[2].

After daydreaming and before going to sleep, I scribbled down on my journal:

'…I'm very happy with the Expedition; we actually have a great time all day long, and so far we get along nicely. Although I know that the road will get increasingly harsh, tougher. We still have to get to López River, perhaps our gateway to the Mitre Peninsula…'

---

2. The 'malones' or raids were sudden attacks by natives on different towns. They usually took cattle with them, and sometimes, women.

DAY 7 Something funny happened to me that morning. I was dreaming that I was on a ship and I heard an alarm clock that would not stop. It turned out that it was my own, in real life, that had gone off who knows how long ago.

I got up and woke the guys up; we started walking at nine twenty. Before leaving, I took with me a good deal of *charqui*. I left a note for Pati – the farmer of whom I will speak about later on - in which I explained to him about our stay in the outpost and our eating some supplies that we had found there.

An hour later, we reached a beach with cliffs. We went down and took a trail that went into the thick forest. We could move forward without much hassle; the road was clear, it was obvious that it was used by cattle quite often. Once out of the forest we had to continue through tall grassland. We went up a small hill and from its top we could see a lighthouse on the shore. It could only be cape San Pío. We confirmed our position, verifying it via VHF with a fishing vessel that was near the coast. We were right; we had reached a place that was an important symbol, not only for us, but also for all other inhabitants of our country, as that geographical feature is the southernmost tip of Argentina.

We had to visit that lighthouse, and make the most of such a lovely afternoon. The sky was a faithful representation of our flag colours[3]; the sea was as calm as a huge pond. The sun highlighted every shape, silhouette and shadow, filling the whole setting with a golden and powerful light. Juan tied the Argentinean flag to a pole and waved it in the air. We started the descent towards the lighthouse, singing the national anthem. Juan, our 'Guinea Pig', was chosen to climb up to where the light was in the tower. At the risk of being called a coward, I confess that, although I tried to go up, fear prevented me from climbing all the way up to the top, since the ladder was old and pretty rusty.

---

3. The national flag of Argentina dates from 1812. It is composed of three equally wide horizontal bands coloured light blue, white and light blue. In 1818, a yellow Sun of May was added to the center.

In that place, the cliffs are steep and make up a rounded coast of singular beauty. From up there, we could hear the sounds that came from the sea lions hundreds of metres below, at the foot of those massive walls. The only way for us to see them was to carefully lean over the edge.

Later on, looking into matters relative to Fuegian toponymy I found out that the cape was named by Lieutenant Juan José de Elizalde in 1791, after the corvette they were using, called 'San Pío', following the naval tradition of giving the last discovered geographical feature the name of the vessel.

The expedition was entrusted to Elizalde by the Viceroy Arredondo and had the purpose of sailing around the coasts of the island of Tierra del Fuego, looking for English settlements, which, luckily, were not found. At any rate, the expedition was of vital importance, as it gathered precious information on the coastal geography of the Island and greatly enriched Fuegian toponymy.

We removed the flag that Juan had hung on the lighthouse and we started to go back up the hill where we had left our backpacks. We had some *mate* over there, enjoying the landscape and relishing one of the last packs of cookies we had.

A little further ahead, during one of our photo stops, we were surprised to see a pack of about ten dogs coming out from the forest, towards us. Together with the dogs, came two riders. They dismounted and introduced themselves. Who could these two 'Quixotes' of Patagonia be? 'Pati' Vargas and 'Correntino'. We could hardly believe it, but it was true. Pati himself, the one about whom we had heard so many things. He invited us to his outpost, which was only a 'while' away. I imagined that by that expression he meant a short while, no longer that twenty or thirty minutes. Stupid me... I am sure that it was hard for him to think in terms of two-legged locomotion instead of four-legged transportation, as his 'while' became two hours of intense march.

His dwelling should definitely not be called a *rancho*. It had a couple of beds, a dining table, chairs and dry logs by the salamander stove. We took our boots off and made ourselves at home. We started drinking *mate* right away, and over the long hours that we did so, we got to know each other. The official *mate* pourer, Juan, kept the round going until it was dinner time.

Pati, as he himself told us, spent most of his time at the rancho where we were, or sometimes at Sloggett Bay, some hours´ riding east. He herded wild animals, and every so often he had to take some of the animals all the way down to Estancia Moat. Correntino used to work crossing Bompland River, at Estancia Puerto Español, across Aguirre Bay. They were simple, authentic and especially generous. Pati must have been about fifty years old, and Correntino thirty-five.

We told them about or goal and Pati told us that he would ride to Lopez River a couple of days later. He advised us to start walking there on the next day and wait for his arrival. Almost with a fatherly attitude, Pati asked us not to cross the river, to wait for them, so that they could take us to the other side on horseback. I do not know if there is such thing as luck, but I am sure there is fate. Perhaps ours was to meet those two fine men in that remote place of the earth.

Pati Vargas and Correntino.

Correntino fixed dinner: grilled meat with an onion and potato stew. It was really heart-warming for me to see the steam and smell the aromas that came out of the big pot he was stirring. We had a great dinner and we even indulged ourselves with some orange juice. Coffee was the last thing we had, and with it we plunged into an interesting after-dinner conversation. For a while we talked over the plans for the next day: we would leave at about noon, because we had to wait for the low tide, which started at eleven, to be able to cross the beach without difficulty, and once we got to the López river outpost, we would wait for our new friends to get there.

That night I felt especially joyous. So far, everything was going according to plan, as expected and, besides, we had met the only two people that lived between Estancia Moat and the Argentinean Navy outpost at Buen Suceso bay. It amazed me that we were in such a desolate place, where only two souls could be found in hundreds of kilometres. I suddenly thought about something that made me laugh: with our presence there, we had just doubled the local population.

DAY 8 I got up early to make the most of that morning. We were not in a hurry; we would head out just after noon. Of course Pati and Correntino were already up by then. By mid-morning Leo made some *tortas fritas*, and I helped him. We prepared a fair amount; after so many days the body starts to crave for a dose of wheat. Meanwhile, Juan recorded everything on video.

At half past one, we left the house and started walking towards the sea. As soon as we could, we went down to the beach. The coast was wild, filled with gigantic rocks that, although still, seemed to watch every step we took, as if to warn us of something that we still did not know.

That afternoon, Leo started to feel an intense pain in his leg. He took a painkiller, but the medicine took quite a while to kick in. That worried me a bit; we were barely halfway and the next part was the hardest one.

One thing that I have not told you yet is that every day, every morning, afternoon or night, we sung as we walked. That cheered us on, united us in perfect harmony. We had a broad repertoire: from rock ballads of the 60's to Argentinean marches. We travelled to the sound of music, of our out-of-tune voices that tried, hopelessly, to make an impression on the great quietness around us.

When we grew tired of our own harsh voices, we listened to the sounds of nature: the soft breaking of waves against the rocks, the hardly noticeable murmur of the streams, the immortal cries of condors and the eternal glory of winds.

Sometimes it was hours before we broke our silence with a word. Each one deep in their own small world, in that world that every soul carries within, filled with intimate feelings, thoughts and memories, hatred and love. During those eternal days, I pondered over existence, life, work and family. I remembered each and everyone and felt them close to me, although they were a thousand kilometres away. It was my mother whom I thought the most of. I owe her not only my own existence, but being who I am today. Because it was that woman who, throughout my life, was always there for me, telling me to go ahead and do whatever deed I set my mind to. And if I ever succeeded in something, if I ever won a few battles, no doubt it is she who deserves to take the credit, not I.

After walking along the beach for quite some time, we took a trail that took us up once again to lands filled with peat bogs and high grass. From a hill, we saw the unmistakable shape of Sloggett Bay. We could see it clearly and it looked just like the satellite picture that we carried with us. It was beautiful up there. The sun was blinding, reflecting on every pond in the vast peat bog.

We moved forward through a small forest and continued along a clearly defined trail. It was more difficult for us to find the way when we walked on peat. But still, we could move without much difficulty until, that afternoon, we got to an outpost buried deep in the forest. It must have belonged to the gold diggers that Pati had told us about. According to his descriptions, we should find another one if we walked for another hour. It was late, getting dark already, and we had to make a decision. Leo seemed to prefer to stay, but Juan and I wanted to go on. If we stayed, we would have to walk to the other outpost early in the morning to wait for the farmers.

We managed to change Leo's mind and continued walking. We redoubled our pace, as it was almost dark by now and we had to get there before the last rays of sun shone us a goodnight.

Sometimes we humans are dumb, stupid and hasty. Our enthusiasm made us walk during the night. Even worse, we did that in uncharted territory. I thank God and our guardian angels for keeping us safe, but I must admit that what we did was wrong. It was careless of us; we answered the call of our passions and not that of reason. In those cases, where actions come from the heart unfiltered by our head, lives usually are put at stake, risks are increased and accidents occur.

We moved increasingly fast on the peat, as it was quite firm. One hour had gone by and the sky was already dark. The refuge was nowhere to be seen. I do not remember who shout it first, but I do remember how loud it felt, breaking the silence of the night: '*Rancho!*'

Inside, we could hear a dog barking. I came close to the door with my flashlight and saw the eyes of the most frightened animal I have ever seen. I went in slowly and the dog quickly hid in the room next door. He was in the corner, facing the wall, head down, much like a resigned prisoner waiting for his punishment. I cut some meat that was hanging from the ceiling and gave it to him. Besides being afraid, it was obvious that he was hungry. Ravenous. When the guys came in, the dog left the house, as if waiving his right to stay there to us.

The place was in fairly good condition; there was an acceptable salamander stove and some stools. We were surprised to find that the glass windows were not broken. But without any doubt, the high point was to find fresh meat. I made us some highly seasoned steaks with soup. Everyone liked the menu.

We stayed by the fire for a long time, telling stories while we drank some *mate*, speaking of life and its winding paths. Before going to bed, we recorded on video our testimonies of the expedition so far.

DAY 9 I had felt like going fishing for a while. We had to wait till the evening for the men on horseback, so that morning was the perfect opportunity to give it a go. With my precarious fishing gear (a tin can, some line and a few hooks), I went to the estuary of the López River. Upon getting there, and very much against my inclination, I had to admit that what we had been told about the river was true to the letter: it is really fearsome. The problem is not its width, but its fast flow, its cloudy and confusing waters. I tried to picture myself crossing the river, and for a few seconds I was breathless. It was not a simple task, especially, with the stories of farmers losing their lives in the very same strong-willed river that I was observing echoing in my mind. What were the odds of us crossing safely when expert farmers had died trying…

I put a stop to my wandering mind and lost myself to the art of fishing for a few hours. I got so lost in myself that I could not catch a single fish. And now that I write about it, I remember the words by my friend Manolo: 'Fishing is like a lady: flighty, elusive, selective and not easy at all.' How much truth I see in those words now!

I still had some time to spare, so I went out to see a gold dredge near the river bank. It is huge. Being on that bay, and seeing that old machinery made me think of the times of the gold rush in Tierra del Fuego; and I could not help but think about Popper and El Páramo, the place where that eccentric Romanian engineer settled down, close to the bay of San Sebastián. I recalled his attempts to build his own empire by means of the precious metal. I imagined his post stamp, his own currency, and his infinite ambitions. Although he was able to extract a fair share of gold, there are so many versions as to the amount that it is hard to tell exactly how much. The truth is that Julio Popper was a visionary and a dreamer, and as is often the case with such people, he has gained a page in the book of history. He is acknowledged as one of the pioneers in exploring the inner part of the island. Thanks to his many incursions, we now call many things the way he decided to name them. The López River is among them. But the most important one (at least to me and this book) is, without a doubt, the Mitre Peninsula. He named it after the then President of Argentina.

Coming back to Sloggett, I cannot fail to mention those who were there. Mainly, the bay was inhabited by gold diggers from Dalmatia, although those shores were also home to adventurers, lonesome men in the hunt for the precious metal. Men who sadly devoted their lives to finding the 'gold vein' and wound up occasionally stumbling into a gold nugget that by no means justified all the sacrifice made to pursue the golden dream. From those days we now only have memories and that rusty dinosaur, the starting point of my little digression into the past.

I decided to go back to the outpost, for my stomach reminded me that it was almost noon. Upon seeing me, the guys asked me if I had caught any fish. I told them the truth, and Juan, changing the wording and meaning of a famous phrase by Napoleon told me: 'Persevere and you shall get

Gold dredge on Slogget Bay.

tired.' It was obvious that the guys would make fun of my attempt at the sport.

Although they had already eaten, they had no problem eating some steaks with me. And I liked that. To kill some time, the three musketeers entered into a fierce aim and shoot competition. At last, I was right: the slingshot did come in handy. Leo was leading followed by Juan. When everything pointed at me losing the competition, I turned the results with my last shot: it was a tied between Leo and me, and Juan was left absolute last. The slingshot broke right after that memorable shot, so the results could not be overturned.

Moments later, the farmers arrived with their horses, followed by a pack of almost twenty dogs. We were ready, so we got our backpacks and started to walk upstream. Following Pati's instructions, we crossed one of the branches of the river with the water up to our knees. Pati crossed at another point that he already knew; the water level there reached his horse's chest. We crossed one at a time, for they had only two horses. When it was Leo's turn something happened that could have

Quixotes of the Patagonia: Pati Vargas and Correntino reaching Sloggett Bay.

had a bad ending. Unwittingly, he poked the horse with one of his walking poles, and made him dash off. Luckily, there were no major consequences.

Once the three of us were safe over the other side, Correntino crossed our backpacks for us, one at a time. Unbelievable! And how incongruous! The toughest river in the whole expedition, we crossed it and we only got wet up to our knees - better even that at Encajonado River. We were all really excited. The Lopez was not just another river in the expedition; it was the portal to the Mitre Peninsula. Somehow, it was like taking an enormous weight off our backs.

We kept on walking, and twenty minutes later we got to an outpost. It looked quite run-down, although the upper floor was alright. It even had three mattresses.

Pati and Correntino lit a fire by the trees. We asked them about which way we should go the next day, so Pati took Juan and me up a hill. From the top we clearly saw the geography of the coast, its shape and features. While he shared his vast knowledge on the characteristics of the land with us, Juan recorded every detail of the situation. It would have been a shame to lose all those words and signs, unique shapes that constituted, no doubt, a valuable legacy. Listening to Pati's teachings was not like reading a history book; even better, it was like living a great deal of it first hand. Every word he uttered confirmed that the traditions and the typical *gaucho* language still survive in some parts of the Argentinean Patagonia.

Later on, I returned to the estuary of the Lopez River but on the opposite bank, to give fishing another go. But once again, my efforts were in vain.

When I came back to the fire, I found all the '*paisanos*' were enjoying some *mate*. By the fire I could see that Correntino was cooking a generous piece of meat. Before dining, we decided to use the sat phone to inform Leo's wife of our position, and give her an update on the expedition. From her home, Ana was responsible for talking to our families, the Coast Guard and the Navy. I would have never guessed that the device

DAY 10 We got up really early. Just before leaving, Pati invited us to eat some steaks (the meat was already cooked and hot for eating) and drink some *mate* to 'get the guts warm', as he used to say to us.

We left the place at about eleven. At least we had already eaten heartily and thus felt content. This was our first bad day. And I say that in the broadest sense of the word, because we got lost several times, it rained heavily and Leo was in a constant bad mood. Juan and I did not pay too much attention to that; we thought it best to let him be and let him find his own peace.

We had a hard time finding the way; at a given point we went too high up and completely lost track of the trail. The ground was very wet and visibility was poor. After wandering around lost in the fog, we decided to go back to the shoreline. We were lucky enough to find a very clear path.

We eventually went down to a beach where we found yellow sand. I had never seen sand of such a colour, and finding it in that strange place in the land of oblivion and the unknown was a very pleasant surprise. Too bad that the day was awful and it was late, so we could neither take pictures or video tape it. Anyway, I believe that the best images are those that we treasure deep in our own memory bank.

Although we would have liked to stay longer in that solitary beach, we had to keep moving. Come hell or high water, we would look for the farmers' trails. We could not find them; we had no idea where they could be. It was late, we could not find the outpost, and we were already resigned to setting up our tent. The day was not favourable, the sky was grayish and the night moved in on us at a fast pace. Just when we were about to give in, I caught sight of the flickering light of a bonfire, deep in the woods. And once again, our ritual: the shout of 'rancho', the group hug and the celebration; a clear victory in the many battles that we had to fight every day. On that same military note, I must say that our strategy for the day really worked, like it did in many other occasions. We kept going despite the obstacles; we never lost faith in ourselves.

The farmers heard us shouting and came out to meet us. Before getting to the refuge, we had to cross another river. The water level was a little higher than our knees. Once on the other side we saw something that seemed quite funny given the circumstances. We were climbing the last hill, and Pati was kicking about a ball that he had found on the shore. The weird thing was that he did so while walking, in the most absolute darkness.

We were happy, tired but glad of having found those fine *gauchos* once again. The refuge was not the best one ever, in fact, it was quite poor. It had just some logs covered with plastic that could never handle the rain effectively. We decided to call the place 'Plastic Rancho.' The highlight was the fireplace. The flames expanded freely between big rocks that somehow reminded me of those big fireplaces that can be found in some houses.

Being with Pati and Correntino was reason enough for us to be more than happy. Leo seemed to be at ease with himself once again and even surprised us by telling some jokes. That cheered me up greatly.

For dinner, we had meat and rice that Leo cooked. For dessert, we had some guanaco[4] meat that Pati's dogs had hunted. I thought that it was going to taste worse that it did. It was alright, although a little rubbery.

We used our tent rain fly as shelter from the rain, which seemed determined to keep falling down all night long. We slept on a bed of logs. As usual, I went to bed earlier. I fell asleep little by little, thinking about nothing, to the sweet sound of raindrops hitting the roof.

---

4. South American mammal (*lama guanicoe*), allied to the llama, but of larger size and more graceful form, inhabiting the southern Andes and Patagonia. It is supposed by some to be the llama in a wild state. In Tierra del Fuego, most of them are found in the center, north and east of the Island.

Ahead of us, the woods appeared as a solid front with no trail, no way out, no clearing. They surrounded us like a wall, everywhere, in any direction, so much so that at times we could not move either forward or backwards..

JULIO POPPER

DAY 11 After some tasty *mates*, we prepared everything for departure. Pati and Correntino would lead the way for some kilometres; then they would return to Sloggett Bay. It was with a heavy heart that I said goodbye to those farmers. They had treated us so pleasantly that it would be hard to part with them. But that was how it had to be; they had to go their way and we had to go ours - different destinations and opposite directions.

We walked with them for almost an hour. Before leaving, Pati gave us the last tips on the terrain. We were about to say goodbye, but almost angrily, Pati said to us: 'Go away, I don't like goodbyes.' I clearly remember his words and the look on his face when he said them. He had a tough and harsh look, eyes set on the horizon, and a gentlemanly stand, that of an unknown adventurer who fights not against windmills, but against the hostility of the weather and the forces of nature. Saying goodbye to those two fine men was a moving scene. We walked a few hundred metres and I looked back to catch one last glimpse of those two riders who had helped us so much over those days, two heroes who dared defy the passing of time and the frontiers of oblivion.

that he himself had taken there. As for his wife, she knitted, took care of the outpost and raised their children. What a brave woman she was, enduring such a life, in a place of such great silence and lonely oblivion!

Such a woman deserved to have homage paid to her, and her husband did so by personally taking the commemorative plaque to San Gonzalo lighthouse, at age eighty eight. I could not believe the story when I heard it. For you to have a more clear idea of his love for his wife, this is the letter that Pedro Ostoich sent in 1994 to the Ministry of the Navy:[1]

'Villa Tesei, October 17, 1994.

Att. Ministry of the Navy,
To whom it may concern:
I hereby request your permission to place a commemorative plaque at San Gonzalo lighthouse, in Aguirre Bay, Ushuaia, Tierra del Fuego.
I would greatly appreciate your accepting this request, as it is my greatest desire to pay homage to the woman with whom I shared my life in these desolate parts, who gave me four children. Being 88, and being humbly grateful to this Ministry, I point out that in 1950 the ship Patagonia, with a very isolated crew, went to Aguirre Bay and San Gonzalo lighthouse to load my wool bales to take them to Buenos Aires, when it was urgent for me to go there because my wife had fallen ill. The plaque reads as follows: 'In memory of the brave first Argentinean white woman, Duisa María Ostoich de Ostoich. Married to the first settler, Pedro Ostoich. Born in Rojas, province of Buenos Aires, died at age 48 in Villa Tesei, Morón, on December 15, 1968, victim of a long disease. Her husband and her four children.'
I appreciate your taking the time to read this and I await you response at your earliest convenience.
I attach photocopies of the Book of the Centennial for you to know why I submit this request.

---

1. OSTOICH, Pedro, *Un Solitario en Tierra del Fuego*, page 87.

*My name is Pedro Ostoich. I live in (...), Villa Tesei,
Morón, Province of Buenos Aires. Best Regards, Pedro Ostoich.*

*PS. The plaque is ready. My wish is to place it there myself.
I would bear the costs of the trip. I only request your authorization.
Thank you very much.'*

Was there a way to say 'no' to such noble deed? When you
find important figures, such as Pedro Ostoich, you feel moral-
ly obliged to acknowledge them because they are the real
heroes who struggled to survive in the wilderness, in the land
of exile with nothing but the bare essentials.

Before leaving that place, I paid my silent tribute to Pedro
and his wife, for having lived there in the way they did.

Then we continued our way north. Just like Pati had told
us, we had to 'cross the Andes.' We started gaining altitude
going through some forests that luckily were not difficult to
cross. After an hour or so, we got to the mountain ridge.
From up there, we could see Aguirre Bay and, most importantly, Estancia Puerto Español. We were happy but could not
stop for long because the cold was giving Juan a hard time
with his feet, and the best way to fight that is to keep walking.
We only paused to drink some hot *mate*. But it was then that
I saw Juan's eyes filled with fear, and I got worried. We had to
keep going through a thick forest and go all the way down to
the estancia.

It was very much like a rainforest. Thousands of *guindos* and
canelos, fallen logs and walls of moss, everything mixed to create a humid and muddy world in which moving was not an easy
task. We decided to follow a nearby stream, where the vegetation was not so thick and we could walk more freely. A guanaco saw us invading his territory and immediately fled the place.

Slips and falls were plentiful, some of them funny enough
for giving the expedition the necessary shot of fun to maintain
a high morale.

Then I felt a cool breeze on my face. It was impossible for
the wind to penetrate such thick forest. So I guessed that we

and Ángel de Andrés. Many of the people who got there arrived by sailboat; other, far more courageous, like Ángel de Andrés, came here on foot.

It was nice to read the comments of people who had already been in this part of the world and learning about their stories, different in many aspects, but with a shared love for nature, for discovering faraway, almost virgin, lands.

I went to bed early despite the fact that we would have time to rest on the next day. I wanted to make the most of my stay there, and I also wanted to visit 'Gardiner's Caves.'

DAY 13   Upon opening my eyes, I saw through the dusty window the pink shades of those dawns that we tend to hold in our memory forever. I had a hearty breakfast and went to the shore with Leo and Juan. We stayed there for a while, in silence, enjoying the warmth of the sunshine, the murmur of the rolling waves and the hollow song of the wind. I would spend the day visiting the caves by myself, for my companions were not willing to go back and cross the Bompland two more times.

I left at noon. It was quite cold, so the idea of walking in icy waters was not a pleasant one. It took me a while to feel warm again. I tried to walk faster and firmly to get the blood pumping, and I put on my gloves and hat. But before going on with my own story I feel I must tell you about the bay itself. Aguirre Bay was named so by Lieutenant Juan José de Elizalde in 1791, after his cousin Pedro de Aguirre. I got most of the information about the area from the experiences told by Pedro Ostoich who, as I told you before, was one of the first settlers of the bay. In 1940, the SADICCAP (Argentinean Society of Industrialization, Trade, Hunting and Fishing, Inc.) settled there. Their founders, Lieutenant Colonel Sánchez Reynafé and Augusto Huber, invested in Aguirre Bay and Thetis Bay. They obtained sea lion fat mostly for tanneries, although some oil was obtained for heavy machinery lubricants. The hides were not very valuable compared to those from other countries, as they were heavily scarred due to the many fights that the animals engaged in.

Stockholders were not convinced by the performance of the business and they put up a fox farm where they kept red, blue, white, cross and silver foxes along with some minks. Some of them were brought from another establishment that they had in the Argentinean province of San Juan while others came from Thiensville, Wisconsin, United States. The venture failed as the animals developed rickets due to poor feeding.

Profitability was far from ideal for these two bold business-men, so they decided to take up new business alternatives, as Pedro Ostoich tells us in his book[4]:

---

4. OSTOICH, Pedro, op. cit. page. 57.

'The fox and mink farm finally failed and they decided to go into the wood business. They set up a traction engine, a circular saw of 1.20 cm of diameter with a four-meter cart and three circular edgers with a power generator for lighting.

They work with lenga wood, producing about three thousand logs per year and they started operating in 1950. (...) They had thirty or forty people working for them, and they were considering the creation of a town. The Navy took the logs to the capital city in their ships, and the trips to Ushuaia were aboard cutter Garibaldi.'

This last venture was also a failure because SADICCAP partners had to cover excessively high costs for the transportation of all the facilities. The loss of many shipments due to bad weather was a major cause of the failure.

It is noteworthy that in 1950 the company built a house that was supposed to function as a police outpost[5]. Some policemen even moved there at the time, but there is hardly any trace of those entrepreneurial endeavours, except for some collapsed wooden structures, rotted by the sea breeze and by the infallible claws of the kings of apathy.

I went into several of those outposts. There was nothing but the awful image of destruction and abandonment, and comments by the travellers that had been there before me. One of the structures had a sign that said 'Capitán Garibaldi.' That was the police outpost that I was telling you about.

While walking along those shores, seeing all of this, I started to think whether those houses should be fixed to be used by travellers, or if they should be left untouched, serving as mute witnesses of history and the passing of time. I did not arrive at a conclusion. I could go on and on dwelling on the pros and cons, but this is not the place for doing it. I must continue with the story and tell you about Allen Gardiner, an English missionary who starved to death at the caves that I now had before me.

---

5. I had the chance to read the book of records of that outpost at the Archives of the Museo del Fin del Mundo (Museum of the End of the World). They show the disembarkation of transports going to Ushuaia, the guard relief, transportation of people, inspection by police officers and news relating to the development of the economic activities of the place.

Captain Allen Gardiner served the Royal English Navy for many years. In 1834, after his wife died, he decided to leave the Navy and devote himself to the Lord and spread the Holy Word, which he did until the end of his days. He travelled the world in pursuit of spiritual conquest. He visited South Africa, New Guinea, Bolivia, Chile and Argentina. He was one of the leading founders of the Patagonian Missionary Society.

Finally, he felt the call to go to Tierra del Fuego. It was only in 1848 that he reached the shores of the island, albeit for a brief period, as he had to return to England due to a shortage of resources and supplies. Two years later, Allen Gardiner and six other men (Richard Williams, John Maidment, Joseph Edwin, John Badcock, John Bryant and John Pearce) set course for the South Atlantic Ocean on board the *Ocean Queen*. They also took two cutters eight metres in length, two boats and supplies for six months.

That same year, on December 5th, they anchored in Banner Bay, on Picton Island. On the nineteenth day of that same month, the *Ocean Queen* departed and left the missionaries on their own. I can picture the scene: the sailors waving goodbye to those men who were making huge sacrifices to spread the word of the Lord. They were the last ones to see them alive.

They found several aborigines of the Yamana tribe who were eager to show their hostility. It was impossible to establish a relationship with them, as they became increasingly aggressive. The missionaries were forced to flee east. They thought it would be difficult to take all their supplies with them because of the weight, so they decided to bury a part of them. They reached Puerto Español, the place that had been chosen by Gardiner for being remote and scarce in resources. He thought that the aborigines would not go to that area; and he was right.

During a strong storm the missionaries left their boats and went into a cavern near the shore. Some days later, they went back to Banner Bay to pick up the supplies that they had hidden and to leave a sign in case a ship would stop by. They buried some bottles with messages in them, where they specified the place where they would be waiting to be rescued. They buried some stakes there and they painted the following in white:

> *Dig Below,*
> *Go to Spaniard Harbour*
> *March*
> *1851*

They went back to Puerto Español. Weather permitting, they stayed on their boats, otherwise, they sought shelter in the cavern. They were running short on supplies and, to make things worse, they had left most of the powder for their guns aboard the *Ocean Queen*; there was no way they could hunt for food.

One by one, they succumbed to a slow and dark death. They would all die and, despite being aware of that unavoidable ending, at no point did they feel disheartened. With the calmness of someone who does things in a relaxed and unhurried way, the missionaries wrote on their diaries. They spoke about their thoughts, their desires, and their last words just before their final breath. Their bodies were falling, one by one, but their souls and their hearts were as alive as ever, faith kept them pure and untouched before dying.

Not as I imagined, reading their diaries is not at all horrifying. Actually, they transmit a serenity that is praiseworthy, like for example Richard Williams when he finishes his last letter saying[6]: *'I am happier than I can express.'*

Gardiner was the last one to die, and he passed away getting from the boat to the cave looking for survivors. His final entry in his diary is worth transcribing[7]:

---

6. BRIDGES, Lucas, *El último confín de la tierra (The Uttermost Part of the Earth)*, Marymar, 1978, Buenos Aires, page 32.

7. CANCLINI, Arnoldo, *Hasta lo último de la tierra*, La Aurora, 1951, Buenos Aires, page 90.

'Friday, September 5th. Great and marvellous is the loving grace of my kind Lord unto me. He has preserved me hitherto for four days, without any food for my physical body and yet with no feelings of hunger or thirst.'

It was only on October 22nd that the sailors of the *John Davidson* discovered the horrific sight. Among them was the then officer Argentinean sailor, Luis Piedrabuena, who later on was to gain world renown as a rescue worker at many shipwrecks.

That was the end of Gardiner and his dream. The evangelizing task in Tierra del Fuego was continued by other missionaries such as Stirling and Thomas Bridges, although not for many years. However, the Yamanas were doomed to extinction.

This extinction is directly related to the arrival of white men in Tierra del Fuego. Although there were no organized mass killings, as with many other ethnic groups in the world[8], the arrival of Europeans led to their complete demise. Firstly, through the arrival on the Fuegian Archipelago of many commercial seal and sea lion hunters, locally referred to as *loberos*, who started to hunt down the very animals that were part of the Yamanan diet. These sea nomads mainly fed on sea lions; they needed them because their meat is rich in fat, which increases the body temperature of those who eat it[9]. We must remember that these aborigines were naked year-round, even during winter.

Nevertheless, the main cause for the almost total disappearance of the Yamanas was the endless introduction of diseases brought by the white man. The difficulty and unwillingness of the Yamanas to adapt their habits to those of the Europeans, and vice versa, contributed to this process. In the words of

---

8. It could be said that persecution and outright murder of natives by Europeans occurred in isolated cases. And as Gusinde notes, there was no reason here to exterminate the first dwellers of the Fuegian Archipelago, as there were no special elements that could be appealing to the white man's greed.

9. The scientists on board the *Mission Scientifique du Cap Horn* (1882 - 1883) proved, through various measurements, that the Yamanas had higher body temperature than average.

someone who had first hand contact with the first nations of Tierra del Fuego[10]:

'*By the time the mission station was built in Ushuaia, the Yamanas had started to die in big numbers. Violent epidemics, which no one could counter, were responsible for destroying the whole town and represented the doom of this tribe. Later on, alcohol was the one element that contributed to the extermination of the group and the adaptation of survivors to the European way of life was the final straw to break their resistance.'*

And in connection with that, in his book Gusinde quotes the words of one of the missionaries in Ushuaia, John Lawrence, who on January 3rd, 1885 asserted that '*from the moment in which the first vessel arrived to these shores, about five or six years ago, natives have been permanently ill: before this time, long epidemics and premature death were very rare.*'[11]

Another negative imposition of the missionaries on the Yamanas was for the latter to wear European clothes. Once again, I will let Gusinde explain this concept to you[12]:

'*Those Europeans who, with best intentions, had provided Fuegians with plenty of clothing, trying to pull them out of their misery, were wrong and did not take into account the natural adaptation of the natives to their hostile environment. Nudity made them incredibly healthy, as their whole body was exposed to the benefits of fire. The protection that the poor European clothes were supposed to deliver was questionable and always hindered by prejudices that ruled out those few advantages. I cannot think of a single true advantage provided by our clothing for those natives, but I can mention many of their previous nude condition in which they remained strong, healthy and happy for centuries.*'

Although perhaps Europeans did not have bad intentions, the contact that they established with the natives generated a negative and irreparable effect, which led to the complete

---

10. GUSINDE, Martín, *Los Indios de Tierra del Fuego*, Centro Argentino de Etnología Americana, Buenos Aires, 1986, Volume II, page 326.

11. LAWRENCE, John, in Gusinde, Martín, op. cit., page 328.

12. GUSINDE, Martín, op. cit., page 336.

disappearance of the Yamanas. But as sometimes happens in the history of civilization, even the best intentions can cause the worst catastrophes.

From all this, it is clear that the Yamanas were not ready to live like Europeans; in fact, their arrival on the Island was absolutely counterproductive. European habits only contributed to the loss of the Yamana identity. As years went by, the development of the mission and, later on, the growth of Ushuaia as an urban center would cause the irrevocable loss of all traces of the existence of the first nations.

Back to my story, I must say that I got as close to the caves as I could but, unfortunately, I could not go inside, because it was high tide and the ocean prevented me from moving closer. My consolation prize was to find a few crosses near the place. Underneath them there were two plaques, one placed there by the Christian Church and the other by the Salesian Mission. They both were in the memory of the martyr Gardiner and his fellow missionaries.

My soul was satisfied; I would have never forgiven myself for being so close and not going to that spot, especially because of the history behind it. The significance of Aguirre Bay and Gardiner's Caves was even recognized by the Argentinean Executive Branch in 1984, when they were declared 'national historic landmark.'[13].

I guess that crossing Bompland River twice was the price that I had to pay for visiting that special part of the world, and I do not think it an exaggeration to state that it was a fair price to pay. When I went back to Puerto Español, I felt at home. I told Leo and Juan about my journey to the caves while we drank some *mate*.

I spent the rest of the day taking pictures and resting. Then we had our literary moment, first we read a book called *The Boots of Anselmo Soria*, which we found in the house and constituted the one and only volume in the bookcase. We

---

13. The decree is number 3806, 1984, and it encompasses Aguirre Bay, including 'Gardiner's Caves'.

then moved onto our traditional *Martín Fierro* and its memorable verses.

In the middle of the night I felt the urge to go to the bathroom. I stepped out, and was surprised to find myself under an unusually starry sky. They seemed like too many for just one sky. It was a sublime sight, millions of glittering white spots contrasting with a bluish background. But those tiny lights were actually pieces of a complex puzzle full of stellar systems and remote galaxies, hundreds of millions of light years from ours.

I wondered if there was life in some point of this ocean of lights. Was there a being in charge of keeping them glittering non-stop? For an instant, as fleeting as the stars that flew through the air, I imagined another soul somewhere in space pondering over that same thing, silently contemplating the blue dome populated with fireflies.

Perhaps our thoughts met somewhere in the universe. I do not know, but to be on the safe side, I waved the sky good night before going back in.

DAY 14 I had a very good night's sleep. We started packing our bags with the first rays of light. During those hours, Leo realized that he had spilled two liters of stove fuel, which meant that we should use it only when strictly necessary. At quarter to one we left Puerto Español, with the promise of returning someday. Soon after departing, we found some destroyed structures. According to the information I had, the buildings had burnt down a few years before, and apparently one of them had been the main house of the estancia. I thought that we were going to have a hard time advancing that day, but we were all surprised to move swiftly forward over a solid path. Before reaching the beacon known as Elizalde, we saw two condors flying near us. It was beautiful to watch them fly silently. Too bad that they vanished too fast for me to get my camera and immortalize the image.

Once we reached the place where the beacon was set (the previous night we had checked and confirmed that it was not functioning), we took a short pause to drink some *mate* and rested for a while. The place was very exposed to the elements and we would have to leave soon, as the autumn wind was getting chilly.

We took pictures of the place and recorded the situation on video. We kept going until we reached a thick wood that we had to cross with much effort. It could have been worse. Once we were back on the beach again, we looked back to look at the place that we had come from. We realized, with a touch of humor, that going into that wood had been unnecessary altogether, for there was another path that was absolutely clear and which we could have crossed. Anyway, we had already crossed the densely wooded obstacle. We kept walking on the beach until, after going over a hill, we saw an outpost. The ritual for those occasions was present, as always, although it was more enthusiastic than usual, as we were not aware of the existence of this outpost. We decided to call it 'Surprise Outpost.' Later on, I found out two things about this refuge: its original name is 'First Outpost' and it was built by Mernies, the owner of Puerto Español. Nevertheless, every time I refer to the house that we found with such happiness and that would provide shelter for us on that autumn night, I use the name that we decided to give it.

Leo was in charge of lighting the fire, while Juan and I looked around for dry wood. Dinner was simple yet tasty and warming - noodle soup. By looking at our supplies, we realized that we were running short, so food became increasingly important over the days. We were physically fine and, more importantly, our hearts were filled with the necessary joy to keep going.

After drinking some tea, a sudden downpour started to fall heavily from the sky. And, in thinking about it, I remember a funny anecdote related to that episode. Now I laugh at it from the comfort of the city, but finding out that only my things (my fellow walkers' clothes were dry) had become wet inside the outpost was, at the time, tragic enough to depress me. It seemed that the rain had conspired with the roof to make my life wet and miserable. It is incredible how time can change your perspective on things; the bitterest moments can turn into the sweetest anecdotes. Just like this one.

Surprise Outpost. Aguirre Bay.

I was about to try to sleep, although I was very annoyed, but the guys cheered me up and invited me to drink some *mate* by the fire. I stayed with them for a while, talking and drying my damp clothes. They passed on their positive energy and thanks to that I found myself at ease and was able to get some rest that night.

DAY 15 The red skies that I had seen that morning made me think that it was going to be a beautiful day. How wrong was I - just before heading out, it started to rain. We had to cross a river shortly after, and my feet got so cold that I could not feel them anymore. They only did what my legs forced them to do; were I to depend on them for moving, I would have stayed right there. My body temperature did not take long to regain stability; in fact, half an hour later we took our warm clothes off, for we were sweating.

Luckily for us, we could follow a clearly marked path all day long. But luck is not eternal, and the clear path also made us vulnerable to the constant rain that fell on us. We were soaking wet, and I badly wanted just to get there. I did not know, nor did I care, where; I just wanted to hide from that overcast sky that did not stop whipping our bodies with mighty drops; I just wanted to stop, rest and take shelter under another unknown Fuegian refuge on the wild coasts of the end of the earth.

It was not long before I spotted a wooden gate, although I said nothing at the time, in case I raised false expectations. We kept going and then there was no doubt. We had reached yet another outpost, 'Pati's bagualero', a refuge that he uses when he herds wild animals. It was actually far from being a palace, but to my by then almost uncritical eyes, it resembled a 19th century Victorian residence built on a hill top overlooking the vast Atlantic Ocean.

I was shivering with cold, so I immediately started to light a fire. I think that Leo and Juan sensed that I had been more affected by the rain than them so they volunteered to search for firewood. It was not easy to get the wet branches to burn, but we persisted and eventually succeeded. We managed to dry up and feel warm once again.

Inside, the refuge was almost destroyed and there were leaks everywhere. Leo and Juan tried to fix the roof, or at least to partially mitigate the constant battering of the rain.

Two miracles happened on that afternoon. The first one was finding a jar full of coffee. The second one is that the clouds vanished, and the sun started to shine brightly.

I tried to communicate with a fishing boat that was near the coast, but our VHF was running low on batteries and I could not transmit the full message. So as not to worry the crew, we called the Coast Guard on our sat phone. We advised that we were fine and asked the officer on guard to pass on the news to Ana, Leo's wife.

It was not easy to make him understand who we were and what we wanted. He eventually understood that we were three madmen who had walked all the way here, trying to tell our loved ones that we were fine through the vessel that was sailing near Punta Colmillo, on Aguirre Bay, right in front of us.

It was that day that Juan thought of a new strategy. We would watch guard on shifts at night time, so that we could keep the fire going to save fuel and depart early the next morning. The place where we lit the fire had no damper, so the room was full of smoke that burnt our eyes. While sitting next to the fire it was alright, but as soon as we stood up it was unbearable. The night grew darker and after our hefty meal, it was time to start our guard shifts.

We talked over how long it would take us to reach Valentin Bay. Leo was the most optimistic. I was more of a conservative in that sense and said that it was going to take us six days to get there. Actually, none of us knew for sure.

I was last to stand guard, from four to seven in the morning. Leo woke me up with a hot tea for me to take over; it was a nice way of starting my shift.

While watching the fire, I wrote in my diary. I guess that the warm glow of those flames in the middle of the dark night inspired me to write these lines that I transcribe for you:

Oh, fire, giver of light,
Giver of warmth,
You, twinkling giver of
The sparkles of joy.

This is an ode to you
Because you radiate power,
You inspire the muses
And you light the hearts.

With your sweet warmth,
You awaken passions
In cold hearts
And rekindle the heat
In dwindling souls.

Oh, fire of millenia
Oh, fire of legends
Your flame casts light
On the way of the devout,
On the path of the good,
On the streak of the ambitious.

Oh, fire of the song,
You have been witness
To a million feelings,
To glee and celebration
And to tears and sorrow.

Oh, devilish fire,
You stir the souls
And turn them red hot,
bursting with excitement.

Oh, fire of the pilgrims,
Oh, fire of the Christian
You bathe in hope
The lives of the poor.

Oh, fire of the traveller,
The mountaineer and the explorer,
Give us the warmth

Of your fervent embrace
And shelter us as a refuge

Oh, fire of the war, of the heated battle,
Of the Crusade and the scrimmage,
Do not shed blood in vain,
Refrain from giving in
To the unfair thirst for vengeance.

Oh, fire of sailors,
Of seafarers and corsairs,
Your face contours the trail ahead
In the shadows.

Oh, fire of the burning embers,
You, fleeting forge,
Your flame shall always feed
The passion of lovers

Oh, you bonfire,
Do not ever die out,
Live on forever,
For as long as you live
Our hearts shall always beat.

DAY 16 We were up by eight. Before leaving, Leo read what he had written during his shift to us. He expressed, in a few lines, how deeply he loved his wife and two kids; he wondered what on earth he was doing there when he felt that he should be with them. He could not bear the weight of his own words; he broke down and started to cry. It seemed like his soul was oozing crystal drops from his watery eyes in streams of tears, so honest that would have moved even the coldest human being on earth.

It was an amazing day, for the sky was absolutely devoid of clouds, and best of all was that the night had covered the soil with frost. You might think that I am crazy for saying this. But it can be easily explained, I am speaking about the firmness of the ground. It was so cold that the soil seemed to be made out of rocks. Unlike other days, we could move forward easily and fast, without sinking in marshy terrain.

Leo complained of a stomach ache right after we started walking. Luckily, his belly got better in no time, but for most of the day he was partially blinded because of the fumes and smoke that had concentrated inside the outpost.

The trail took us deep into the forest. Sun rays filtered through the tree branches, which somehow made the whole place look mysterious and revealing. I do not know if I could understand its mystery; but I am sure that it was one of the most beautiful scenes that nature has revealed to me so far. I swear that no artist could have captured the beauty of the bucolic image that I had in front of me.

We found a path that enabled us to move easily through those magical forests. During one of our stops, we ate the last bits of chocolate that we had. We were sure going to miss it!

The winding path finally took us to the beach. It was a real pleasure to walk on that hard sand, it almost felt like pavement. Soon after we reached a refuge that was almost run-down. We did not throw a party upon finding it, since we were going to stay there for a short while, just enough to replenish our energy and keep going. We thought that it should be the last outpost in the 'Pati Estate.' We invented situations, characters and stories weaving figments of our imagination. It was natural for us to do that; after living together for sixteen days, our conversations were starting to focus merely on technical aspects related to paths and courses, task allocation and advance methodologies.

It was funny to think that Pati had created an Empire and that he was the undisputed master of the coasts of Tierra del Fuego. My mind was flooded with images of maps made by mysterious cartographers that showed the vastness of the Emperor's lands. I could picture the mapmakers in my head, secretively putting away all that precious information in unbreakable chests. But like all other big empires in the history of men, the 'Pati Estate' slowly but relentlessly started to fall into decay. That meant that his dreams of conquest would vanish and, in time, all the villages and centres that concentrated the infinite power of the monarch would disappear too, under the implacable yoke of Mother Nature. There we were, right in the last stronghold of what had been, at one time, the 'Pati Estate.'

As soon as I finished the journey inside my fable, I violently clashed with the geographic reality of the place. We were almost at the end of Aguirre Bay, facing Cape Hall. It was there that we took a very important decision for the expedition. Instead of following along the coast, we decided to walk through the valley of 21 de Febrero River . It was the first time that we would leave our major point of reference – the ocean. Choosing that option meant having to put into practice all our knowledge and expertise on map reading and orientation. It would be a great challenge that would require for us to be alert and in full use of our senses.

We decided to change our route because of the difficulties presented by the terrain. A friend of us, Sergio Anselmino, had told us that the coast from Aguirre to Valentín Bay was rough and steep, and that it was difficult to walk there. We agreed that walking along the inner valleys would be easier - at least, we would not bump into those cliffs. We would run the risk and make our own road, also trying to save a few days.

But before going on with my tale, I feel obliged to tell you a little bit about Sergio Anselmino's journey. On April 2004, this unknown gentleman walked from Ushuaia to Río Grande for forty five days without ever leaving the coast. Of course, I must highlight that he accomplished that feat in absolute solitude. And I should add credit to his deed by stating that he was not favored by running into the farmers of the south of the Island that we met during our trip.

I doubt whether I would have been able to finish that journey alone, as Sergio did. Not only because of the loneliness, but also due to his having to carry much more gear; we were three and had the chance to evenly distribute the weight on our packs.

In that expedition, Anselmino discovered the southernmost rock caves in the world. They total fourteen and they vary in depth; most of them are about a hundred and fifty metres deep. I find it amazing that even today, in the 21st century you can still discover something that big. Because of this, every time I speak about Sergio Anselmino, I do so with respect.

That afternoon we saw the first cows since Remolinos. We also saw wild bulls and, although they were at a safe distance, we could clearly sense their strength and great size. We kept moving until we got to the 21 de Febrero River. We crossed it a few hundred metres upstream from our contact point. This time it was Juan's turn to play guinea pig. I thought that it was going to be deeper, but luckily enough the water level was not higher than our waist. Juan got his camera wet, but it did not get damaged.

Leo still had some problems with his eyes, but we had to keep on walking. We continued our journey, always walking along the river bank. We reached a clearing where we stopped to take some pictures of some mountains that, although far off, stood out for their height and snow-capped peaks. They were Pirámide, Campana and Atocha. Although none of them is higher than a thousand metres, their shapes are majestic. We found a forest full of *ñires* there, which was surprising in itself.

We had already lost hope of finding that species, so it was a nice change from the green foliage of the *guindos* and *canelos*.

We decided to look for a place to spend the night a little further ahead. We found another clearing about thirty minutes later. We set up our camp there, just where the river met a little stream. We made Leo stay inside the tent because his eyes were still bothering him quite a bit.

As usual, I made the mistake of not changing my damp clothes to light the fire. I felt my whole body soaked in water, my fingers and toes were already numb, and I had a hard time moving them. The branches were wet and frosted, which turned my attempts to setting them on fire into embarrassing failures. Despite the many attempts, I could not get them to catch. To top it off, I was annoyed by a bull that was nearby, watching us in a weird way. It had a huge head, and that was reason enough to make me nervous. From the noises it made and the way it looked at us, it seemed to be unhappy about our presence. There was no doubt that he wanted to go through the place we were occupying. Luckily, half an hour later, the animal moved on and I could resume my attempts to light the fire.

I was trying so hard and was so concentrated that the next thing I knew was that two hours had gone by. I would have never guessed that seconds and minutes could go by so fast. It seemed as if time was much shorter than normal, that someone was fast forwarding my watch, moving the hand faster to make time rush on. I had tried every trick in my book. I used more wicks than usual; I distributed the branches in every way I could think of, to no avail. There was no fire and my hopes were coming down like a card castle swept by a gust of wind. Juan had come out of the tent to cheer me up, but his faith in our success was also dying, little by little, just like the feeble flames on the wannabe bonfire. I remember telling Juan to be calm, that it was going to get going. It was time to resort to the ace up my sleeve, calling the gods. I started shouting in a way that for sure had nothing to do with Greek ceremonies, calling for Aeolus, the keeper of the winds.

My shouts were suddenly carried further by a developing breeze that started blowing from the woods, and which also miraculously caused the embryonic fire to flare up. To our amazement, it started to grow before our eyes until it looked healthy. The logs were burning fervently, while Juan and I threw in more wood. After two hours of freezing in front of a tiny pile of wet branches, we got the fire going, and we were sure happy about it.

Juan put the kettle on some rock near the fire, and when the water got to the boil, he started shouting 'it boils!' in a weird and happy voice, as if confirming a millennial prophecy. I found it funny; he acted like a kid who got some candy or was given a new toy. We drank tea, *mate* and coffee, we dried our clothes and, finally, we warmed up next to the much loved fire after so many kilometres of walking in damp and cold clothes.

I do not know if the fire got going because of my absurd invocation or by mere luck. The fact is that from that day onward I started asking Aeolus to get my fires going.

Leo Fernández and Federico Gargiulo crossing 21 de Febrero River.

Regretfully, we could not stay for long by the fire, because, as usual, the rain came to put an end to our party. At any rate, we had already accomplished our goal: we had eaten, drunk warm beverages and, the best of all, we had comforted our spirits.

DAY 17 After having breakfast and organizing our gear, we started yet another day in our journey. Thank God, Leo was in perfect shape once again.

From the moment that we decided to go into that valley, our orientation was not based on the sea but on 21 de Febrero River. The first few hours were not very complicated, save for some parts where we had to cross some thick *ñire* forests. We did not worry; we were like a train that defied speed and time, moving on rails that would take us to uncertain destinations, destinations that, ultimately, prove either our victories or our miseries.

Our path that day was determined by the shapes and contours that the river had carved in the ground thousands of years ago. I still think about that watercourse, it got under my skin. Perhaps it is because we had to cross it many times. We did not do it out of whim or because we were mad about the icy waters, but because the opposite bank offered an easier ground for walking. Each time we went into that watery torment I felt like thousands of sharp knives dashed for my skin. Luckily, those imaginary wounds healed shortly after resuming our walk.

At noon we stopped, as usual, and we drank a tasty and warming coffee and some *mate*. We were in a really good mood that day; we even told and played jokes on one another. After the short stop we saw a bull that fled upon seeing us. For a moment, I thought that it had vanished, until I saw it behind some trees. We had no choice but to walk near the beast, because we were flanked by the river and the forest, which left no room to walk at a distance. I had decided that I would jump into the river should that lonesome guardian attack us. But we got lucky once again and the bull just watched us while we crossed in front of him.

Later on, we went into a place that was inhabited by beavers. We knew this by the hundreds of small pointed cut-off trunks that we could see. Having mentioned beavers, I must say that they are not part of the native wildlife of Tierra del Fuego. They were brought from Canada by the Argentinean

Navy in 1946 with the purpose of developing a fur-trading industry, which ended up in an absolute disaster. In their country of origin, the low temperatures make the beaver fur develop outstandingly and turn the pelt into a highly valuable trade item. The temperature in Tierra del Fuego is not that low, hence the fur does not grow as much, rendering the pelt low in value as a trading item.

Because of their genetic characteristics, beavers build dams as defence from their natural predators – bears, wolves and lynxes, none of which exists on the Island. The dams constitute physical barriers that create vast water lakes along the rivers, where these clever creatures (with the aid of branches and mud) build their lodges, which are accessible only to them through underwater entrances. Regarding their impact on the ecosystem, we have to say that rivers overflow as a result of this damming, and consequently the surrounding trees end up drowning.

Currently, beavers are a pest which is very difficult to counter in Tierra del Fuego. I think that if something as well balanced and perfect as Mother Nature was created by a superior being, we humans should at least try to focus on preserving that harmony and should use our energy in something other than altering it by introducing foreign species or plants into ecosystems they do not belong to.

At about four in the afternoon, we decided to call it a day. We had found a nice spot for camping and we just had to cross the river. We were past caring about getting wet, so we crossed without complaints. We even did it with grace and enthusiasm.

As usual, Leo and Juan put up the tent while I set myself to bring light and warmth to the mysteries of the night. I am sure that all the creatures that inhabit the forest observed, in awe, the dance performed by those colours and sparks. It was easy to light the fire this time. We had plenty of *mate* and talked for a long while. We had walked a lot that day, but we did not know for sure if we were moving in the right direction. We missed our families and our loved ones, but that day I realized that I was missing something more immediate, I was thinking about our guide since the beginning of our pilgrimage; I wanted to see the ocean once again.

DAY 18 After our morning routine, we headed off once again, and as every day, we ventured into a new world to discover all sorts of stories. And speaking about stories, that day started with us walking along the same river for a while, and then changing our direction to go southeast, looking for higher ground going up a hill with clear sides which let us move with no difficulty. It was not that high, but the slope was long enough for us to start feeling the physical strain.

Then we saw, yet again, the Pirámide, Campana and Atocha mountains, although this time they were much closer. They looked somewhat threatening now; we felt their presence. When we finally reached the top of the hill, we found a plateau, surrounded by small peat lagoons and by the magnificent shapes of the mountains. But the highpoint of that view was, beyond doubt, to see the pure and immense blue ocean once again. This meant the absolute confirmation that we had walked in the right direction, efficiently following our own set route. This called for a celebration, so the fact that we had enough coffee for a last round of the black brew was exactly what the occasion was calling for.

We kept on moving, with renewed energy. After crossing a gully full of thick vegetation, we reached a point from where we could see a bay. At first we thought it could not be Valentín; we had only walked for two and a half days since we left 'Pati's bagualero'. We started considering that possibility, and despite our doubts and uncertainty we concluded that we were not wrong and that we were really close to Valentín Bay. From where we stood we could clearly see its long beaches and the two rivers that flow into the ocean, the Carabelas and Sudamérica. We thought it impossible for our manoeuvre to have been so successful, flawless. A job 'well done', we could call it. And this meant not only having been successful in walking on route, but also in keeping our team spirit in top shape.

With the excitement that we gradually gained from the magical moment when we saw the shore, once again we violated the law of the hiker, challenging nature and risking our lives. It was five, it was already getting dark; the bay was not far, but we still had to cross a very thick forest. We could not resist the temptation of walking on sand that night, and as a result, we let our hearts rule our heads. Juan lead the way, surely with heavenly aid (I prayed a lot that day), and we managed to move through those colossal *guindos* and *canelos,* and to overcome fallen logs and branches that whipped us as we went by. The great effort and our madness finally paid off. We reached our much-wanted goal, one of the few sand beaches on the southern coast of Tierra del Fuego.

Darkness was almost absolute by now, and we could not admire the beauty of the bay with our eyes. We could, though, get to know it through our other senses. I let myself be taken over by the humid breeze that came from the rolling waves, which, judging by their sound, seemed to break powerfully against the shore. Of course, I grabbed some sand in my hands, and let it slip, as endless as time, through my fingers.

We set up our camp, and I decided to light a mighty fire. The pale flames lit our faces showing the happiness that we had regained after some rather dark days and that, somehow, we felt relaxed enough to express freely, having accomplished part of our overall mission: a part which though small in comparison with the full adventure, to us felt specially significant at the time.

The whole scene was pleasant, both to our eyes and ears. The sweet and warm light cast by the fire that disappeared into the darkness, the cracking sounds of the branches being eaten up by the fire, and the clapping of the waves being carried away by the winds. I sometimes try to relive the magic of that moment, but I cannot. Only a few times have I been able to feel those feelings all over again, but not while awake, always in my dreams. Little by little we moved on from places, treasuring them in some special place in our memory, closing chapter after chapter in a fairly long story, a story that had many blank pages waiting to be filled with the roads and crossroads that the 'Nomads in Mitre' would encounter.

DAY 19 On that particular day, we decided to sleep in for a bit. We had breakfast with no rush whatsoever and we talked extensively before leaving our sleeping bags. It was not long before I started to feel the urge to get to see the bay, so I got up. About this bay I must comment that it was named after Valentín Jansen, the Dutch pilot of one of the vessels of the expedition of 1619 by the Nodal brothers, about which I will mention later on.

Out of all the bays that I was lucky enough to get to know in Tierra del Fuego, Valentín is among those that I remember the most. Perhaps it is because of its beautiful beaches or because it reminds me of the place where I was born, the city of Mar del Plata.

The sandy area of the beach is about five kilometres long and, as I said before, it is interrupted by the estuaries of the Carabelas River and Sudamérica River to the east. As the day was gorgeous and taking advantage of the morning light, I decided to capture the moment and the beauty of those places with my camera. While I walked along the vast sandy beach, besides looking for the perfect image, I picked up seashells, one for each loved-one back home. Souvenirs there remain unchanged by time, pure and intact as when they were created, mementos that truly come from the Earth.

Juan joined me on the beach, and we went back to the campsite where Leo was still resting inside the tent. The three of us put the tent away, and then I poured us some tea while we finished organizing everything. Before leaving the place, Juan decided to share with us some things that he had written the night before. He spoke mainly about the relationship he had with his father, and I could tell that he was having a hard time fighting the tears that threatened to pour down from his moist eyes. We departed shortly after noon, and it was an hour later that we reached Sudamérica River. Crossing it was not a nice experience. Its bed, or at least the part where I crossed it, was very soft and with each step I sunk in deeper, so it was very difficult to move forward. I felt trapped by invisible hands that wanted me to stay there forever. Once on the other side, we saw a refuge that had been built by the Museo del Fin del Mundo. There was a sign put up with its name: 'El Primer Valentino.' It had been built to host archeologists who, once in a while, went to that bay to research the old Haush settlements that could be found in the area. Not a lot of things are known about the Haush, although their habits are thought to have been quite similar to those of the Selk'nam (a.k.a. Onas). Unlike the Yamanas, the Haush were hunters on the land and fed mainly on guanacos. Some people think that they were a minority group of Onas who, for some reason, had been cast away to the east. That is the reason why they are also known as 'Eastern Onas.' The settlements are still under study, because there are many unknown facts about the people who lived there. The latest findings of human remains determined that they were 6,000 years old.

We went into the outpost and we immediately realized that it was in perfect condition but for one thing, the salamander stove. The incident that took place in 'Pati's bagualero' was still fresh in our minds, and unluckily in Leo eyes, so we were a little sensitive about the subject. The stove must have existed at some point in time, because there was a place set aside for lighting a fire, and on top of it there was a round hole for the chimney.

That was the second place were we found a logbook. Juan started to flip trough it and read aloud the parts that had been written by people we knew. Before we realised it, it was already three in the afternoon. It would not pay off to keep walking for just a couple of hours, for darkness would soon force us to camp and we would not go much further that day. We thought that the best decision would be to stay there and spend the night under a roof. We would get up early instead. While we read the logbook, we drank some *mate*, and on those yellowish pages we found the testimonies of some people who had walked the same way that we were planning to go on the next day. We wanted to head northeast, through the valley of Sudamérica River, and try to climb the Negros mountains. Once up there, we would descend towards Buen Suceso Bay. The comments by previous visitors were not an encouraging piece of news. Of course, we also found comments by the omnipresent Ángel de Andrés. He had been here many times, on different occasions with different students of his. Leo, Juan and I talked about the possibility of meeting this man, who seemed to be so famous in the Mitre Peninsula, upon our return to Ushuaia. It would surely be an enriching experience. We were quite sad when we found out that Ángel de Andrés had died only a few years ago.

We felt so at home at 'El Primer Valentino' that we hardly went outside, just to pick up some firewood and water. Before going to bed I wrote a few lines on the logbook under the pale candlelight. They were a summary of our expedition from the beginning to that day, so I think it is worthwhile including them here, besides, they convey my feelings in their most pure and true state, right where they were born, in those solitary infinite beaches, in the anonymous kingdom of winds, solitude and silence:

'May 19th, 2005

After eighteen long days walking, we reached Valentín Bay from Ushuaia. Seeing the bay from those hills was amazing. We left Pati's bagualero at Aguirre Bay only three days ago. We decided to follow 21 de Febrero River until after a day and a half we went up the hills for a better view. Once there we saw the sea, and that was the most encouraging feeling ever, for after three days of not seeing the big blue, we missed it badly. We were forced to go back down and up again through a small yet thick guindo forest. We were so excited that we crossed it in the blink of an eye despite the many obstacles we found. After a couple of hours we climbed back up once again and from there we saw what we thought was Valentín Bay, although we were not sure. I sped up and together with my two co-adventurers, Juan Manuel

Ronco and Leo Fernández, we realized that we were right. The bay's shape, the two rivers flowing into the ocean, the vast sandy area were more than enough to identify our objective. It was already five in the afternoon and despite the imminent darkness, we decided to move on. We wanted to step on that sand, feel the reality of what I now think of as our personal victory. We had to face a kind of rainforest (as Leo described it) made up by guindos and canelos. Juan led the way through the thick forest in the most absolute darkness. I prayed for God to lead us safely to the bay. And He made sure of that, for we got there and stepped on the sand, as we wanted. We were all very happy. We set up the tent by some trees and I lit a fire. Everything was positive that night, the fire, the moon, the place and above all, the satisfaction of knowing that we had reached the bay in only three days, following our own route, the three of us analyzing the options and looking for the best alternative.

Today, May 19th, we reached the refuge and decided to stay here, spend the night and depart early in the morning towards Buen Suceso Bay. We still have a long way to go; our goal is to get to Estancia María Luisa. I do not know whether it will be easy or not, but I have confidence in me, my partners and, besides, I feel that we have been a group at all times. I feel the support of my family, my friends and lots of people who helped us, in some way or another, to accomplish this goal, to go through with this odyssey that we thought of back in October 2004. I am also excited about what is coming next: getting reunited with my loved ones, sharing this story, reliving the bittersweet moments with the people I love the most. Another thing that gets me going is the second stage of this project: speaking about our adventure at the schools of Tierra del Fuego. We want to pass on our love of nature to all the kids, and tell them about the places that exist in our province. I would like to see more people embark on this adventure as we did, because I think it is absolutely fascinating.

I cannot leave out all those people who helped us: the people from the Coast Guard (outposts Moat and Almanza), Juan Carlos and Ramona in Harberton and Pati and Correntino. It is people like them that make me believe, more than ever, that I live in a wonderful country.'

DAY 20 That night was one of the few that I was cold. No matter what I put on, I still felt like my legs were stuck in the deep ice of the last glaciation. The only way to warm up a bit was to wake up every so often to rub one foot against the other.

We tidied up the refuge and left early in the morning. As soon as we started walking, we found many guanacos that stopped running to examine us at a distance. At first we headed north, then we changed our course and headed northeast. The vegetation made it difficult to advance, but we managed all right. In one of our stops, Juan took his backpack off to explore the area more easily. Something happened just then that could have been a serious incident: Juan's backpack fell off and started rolling down a fairly steep hill. Quick on his feet, Leo chased after it down the hill. Luckily enough he did not get hurt and the backpack ended up falling in a stream, so that the only consequence was that his things got a little wet.

Soon after, we reached the timberline. From there we could see the cold waters of Le Maire Strait to the east and the Atlantic Ocean to the north and south. Being on that spot made me realize that I truly was on the peninsula. The day was amazing; the sun bounced off some natural water tarns and gave the whole scene a mystifying hallo. To the southeast, we could see the shape of the beautiful Valentín Bay and, a little further, the ever-captivating Campana, Pirámide and Atocha mountains, which showed behind a giant cloud. We stopped there to catch our breath and drink some instant soup. We took out the Argentinean flag to immortalize the moment with the national emblem as a backdrop. I remember that we started to joke around and imagine what we would have for dinner that night, as we took for granted that we would reach the Navy's outpost.

We headed off right away, since we did not want to be late for dinner. We kept on walking, on hard ground this time, following the guanaco trails that we found. But soon after an hour, a cloud covered the sky and made it impossible to see, disorienting us so badly that we could not advance any further.

It was cold and the night was near. We had no choice but to look for shelter under the trees and, thus, give up our idea of getting to the Navy outpost of Buen Suceso Bay. We could not have chosen a worse place to stay for the night; the soil was soft and damp. The tent hardly fitted between the trees, in a clearing filled with logs, moss and mud on an uneven surface.

The wet branches were a clear sign that that night we would have no fire. Anyway, I tried for over an hour, but I was unable to set the wood on fire. Leo tried to help, but to no avail.

We went back inside the tent, cold and with a low morale, for we had got unnecessarily excited by creating hopes and intentions unsupported by the reality of the trail. We were already inside the sleeping bags and none of us even hinted at wanting to go out and getting some water to cook something. Little by little, silence invaded the tent and drowsiness invaded us; we fell asleep, with the bitter feeling of not having met our expectations.

DAY 21 In order to cheer up, that morning we decided to have a double-sized breakfast. We had not dined and we had a long day ahead of us, for sure. We headed off quite late, at twelve o'clock exactly. We started to gain altitude by walking uphill with difficulty through the forest. We reached a point when we could not go on walking. We were trapped by hundreds of *ñires* that prevented us from going on. Although the forest was low, it was so thick and hard that despite our efforts, it was almost impossible to move. I had never been in such a desperate situation before. It was like being immobilized by thousands of iron arms, arms that would not give in to our wish to succeed. While inside the hideous confinement, I think I understood how people who suffer from claustrophobia feel. We were all very frustrated. Leo hit the branches with fury but was unable to break them, while I tried to move the trees to advance at least an inch, but I just drained my energy in pursue of a goal that seemed unreachable. Like insects caught off guard, we were prisoners trapped in a cobweb, although this cobweb was not made of fine threads but of an intricate maze of branches and logs.

It took us about one hour to make one hundred metres. As soon as we escaped from that wooden nightmare, we heartily and openly cursed all the sub Antarctic forest. It was the easiest and safest way to get it off our chests. The weather that day had been amazing, but soon after exiting the forest the sky became overcast and we were unexpectedly under a heavy snowstorm. We were, once again, left blind, with no reference points. We kept on walking and after a while we spotted the ocean. We did not know where we were, but finding our special friend once again cheered us up. The place was too steep to descend, so we had to retrace our steps and find a place to camp. Our hopes got darker with the vanishing lights of dusk; another day was coming to an end. We decided to set up the tent on the rocky ground that was beneath us right then and there because it was already too late to go back into the forest. We put some big rocks to pin the tent down in case the wind got worse, which was more than likely; we were in the open and we wanted no more surprises. While we were putting our things inside, I realized that I had lost my thermal rest. It was not hard to guess were, it surely was left behind as an offering to the wretched forest. But it was not as bad as it looked, because Leo lent me one of his own. They were very thin, so he had decided to bring two to the adventure. It was that kind of solidarity that many times helped us through tough situations. We had to break the ice layer that had formed over the nearby pond to get some water. Our morale was still fairly low; we had been wandering aimlessly for two whole days on the mountain range, without knowing where we were heading.

After dinner we shared a can of pâté for dessert. To cheer up, we decided to treat ourselves to a film show. From our sleeping bags we enjoyed some of the images that we had shot so far. They were just a few days old, but I already felt that they had been shot a long time ago - López River, the farmers, Gardiner's Caves and Puerto Español. Seeing ourselves in those dream landscapes was like reading a fascinating book and the best of it was that it had been written by us, paced to our rhythm and our own style. I prayed to God that on the next day I could write a few lines about the happiness that we felt upon reaching Buen Suceso Bay. Almost all of our clothes were wet, we were running short on food and we needed to rest for a couple of days. We were both physically and emotionally tired. Little by little, I dozed off by the light of the images that flickered in the tent, until I fell sound asleep.

DAY 22 Getting up and putting on our damp clothes was torture. The absolute worst were the boots, my feet were very cold and I had to walk about for a while to warm them up a bit. At least we had some fun when we saw Juan's beard with a frost. That mat of ice and hair reminded me of a picture I saw in a book about Ernest Shackleton's expedition to Antarctica. There was a picture of a sailor showing his beard aboard the *Endurance*, which looked just like our partner's.

It was an awful day, it was snowing lightly and visibility was very poor. We started to walk the mountain, guided only by our intuition because it was impossible to determine where we were heading on a day like that. There were no different colours, just a disheartening pale and monochromatic shade of gray. We looked at our compass; we studied the sat picture, although we knew that none of that was of any use. We were lost beyond doubt. We moved blindly forward through woods and valleys. We just had to find the trail that would lead us to Buen Suceso Bay. We tried to compass our way out of the spongy soil and thick vegetation, but we ended up walking in circles. We decided to walk along a stream that we run into. We guessed that it had to flow into the shore somewhere. We did not know where, but it was far better than walking without a real reference point.

We followed it for hours, stepping over fallen logs, being whipped by flexible branches and under the eternal leaves of the *guindos*. We reached a clearing, and from there Leo and Juan swore that they saw Buen Suceso Bay. Straining our eyes, Juan made out the unmistakable red of the Navy outpost. Not that I did not trust my partners, but I wanted to keep on walking because, as I was not wearing my glasses, I could not see the refuge with my own two eyes. A few metres further up the hill - and with my glasses on - I could clearly see the bay and the outpost that we had dreamed of so often during the past two days. We felt deliriously happy. We just had to walk through a forest, which was not an easy task but to us seemed like a walk in the park on our way to paradise. It is amazing how your mood can change the perspective of things. The dark hallways of hell can turn into the golden gates of heaven. Or the other way around...

Once we cleared the forest, we had to cross through an area filled with dams, water lakes and logs felled by beavers. It looked like it was their main place of operations. Those were our last steps before reaching the ultimate glory, stepping on the blessed sand of Buen Suceso Bay, and we felt moved by the moment. I could not help my eyes from getting moist, but I hid those tears under my tough man façade. I do not know why, I just did not want Leo and Juan to see me crying. I wiped my eyes with my coat and we started celebrating, taking pictures to record the moment when the 'Nomads in Mitre' went along the bay. Of course we did not forget about our symbol, and once again we took out the Argentinean flag that accompanied us everywhere, which we used to celebrate the great moments in our expedition.

With a solemn attitude we started walking towards the outpost, over the last few metres that separated us from the Paradise that we had been dreaming about for the last few days. We did not bother stopping at the outpost 'Luis Pedro Fique'; we already knew about its existence but we were not sure about its location. We just looked at it out of the corner of our eyes. We did not want to delay any longer the arrival at the Navy outpost where so many delicacies awaited us. There was no one outside, but the loud music coming from a depot that looked like a workshop confirmed something that we were expecting to find there: human life.

A Navy officer called José Manuel welcomed us warmly. He invited us to take our boots off and go inside. He offered us something hot to drink. Leo and Juan chose the traditional *mate* while I decided to deviate from Argentinean tradition and have a cup of coffee with milk. I really needed it. I do not remember whether José invited us to eat the tempting cake that was on the table before or after we had it in our mouth. We then met the other people who lived there. They all turned out to be wonderful. The ice broke as fast as lightning, and soon after arriving we felt like we were longstanding friends. We offered them some cheese and ham that we had brought, and a much-appreciated bottle of wine. We toasted to the happy encounter and, perhaps, to a well deserved rest.

I had never felt that taking a shower was such a big thing as that night. Ordinary things, like a shower, a pastry or some juice were suddenly magical treats with enormous value to us. We humans are like that - we only appreciate things when we no longer have them. That is why I think that, once in a while, it is good to feel that something is missing. That is the only way in which we can see the real value of everything around us. In other words, I think that taking some distance from things does not make us forget about them, it makes us love them even more. In that sense, I must admit that it was good for me to get away from civilization and the world for a while, to get lost in those timeless spaces and travel around the end of the earth.

It was getting dark, which meant that it was dinnertime. Dinner for me was quite strange, because I could not finish the pasta that José Manuel put on my plate. After so many days of eating only once a day my appetite had diminished. Out of pride I tried to finish the tempting pasta that seemed so inviting with its intense contrast between the red sauce and the white plate. Despite my best efforts, I barely ate half of it.

After dinner, it was time for sports. It was the 'Nomads' against the Navy team at table tennis. Leo and Juan represented our team, while I supervised the match from the comfort of a sofa. The adventurers, just like throughout the whole trip, proved to be courageous and brave. But despite their tenacity and efforts, the military tactics prevailed over the tired challengers, and the representatives of the Argentinean Navy won in a tight score. We finished the night watching some movies that we found there. Before going to bed, I wrote all the things that had happened on that day. This is what I wrote; reading it you will get a sense of how I felt regarding the trip so far and what I expected for the rest of the trip:

'It was actually a long and hard way, but, luckily, we managed to cover it losing only my thermal rest and two liters of fuel. We are alive, healthy, and ready to keep on exploring the Mitre Peninsula, no matter what obstacles we find on the way. That is the most important thing, the greatest goal of the expedition: for each and every one of the members of the team to be healthy and well.'

DAY 23 I got up at ten, when I could not sleep anymore. Waking up to no alarms, not shivering from cold and feeling relaxed seemed like a totally new sensation. It was also a rarity to wake up and have chocolate milk with freshly baked home made bread for breakfast. And the best of it all was that there was no need for us to carefully divide the food in equal shares.

It was a beautiful morning, so I went outside to explore the shore of Buen Suceso Bay. I decided to visit the 'Fique' outpost[14]. I went inside and took a quick look. Overall, it was in good condition, although I did not pay attention to details; nothing could be better than the warm and comfortable military outpost.

While I walked on this sandy beach, I could not help but think about Anne Chapman, an anthropologist I had read about before departing. Her story caught my attention because she had walked the same shores that we were walking on now, but back in the '70s. The adventurous researcher had started her journey at Estancia María Luisa, exactly where we were going to finish ours. Anne Chapman recorded several interviews with Ona and some Haush natives, which contributed with lots of information about the anthropology of Tierra del Fuego.

As a tribute to this great woman I transcribe some words she wrote about Buen Suceso Bay and its shape[15]:

'The bay is shaped like a square with a missing side, a dark forest covers the sides and the beach has black rocky outcrops on each end. Inland, the beach turns into a swamp filled with high reeds.'

I would not be able to describe it in a better way. Her words are a true reflection of what my eyes saw there.

---

14. That outpost was built by the Museo del Fin del Mundo as part of the support infrastructure for the *Proyecto Extremo Oriental del Archipiélago Fueguino* (PEOAF) *[Easternmost Fuegian Archipelago Project]*. It was used by the many expeditions that formed part of that project, as well as by the groups from the Salesian Agrotechnical School led by Ángel de Andrés.

15. CHAPMAN, Anne, for the Magazine Karukinka 3, page 12.

I continued exploring my memories and remembered the vessels on which the Nodal brothers sailed back in 1619. I pictured images of those trips; I could clearly see those two brave Spaniards, Gonzalo and Bartolomé, on board their ships, *Nues-tra Señora del Buen Suceso* and *Nuestra Señora de Atocha*, together with the famous cosmographer Diego Ramírez de Arellano. They had departed from Lisbon by the end of 1618 to explore the straits of Le Maire and Magellan. They crossed the Atlantic to get to the shores of Brazil. For a long time, they sailed southbound until they reached the Strait of Magellan. They could not go through it because of the strong winds, so they continued along the northern shore of Tierra del Fuego until they reached the Strait of Le Maire, on Saint Vicente's day, so they decided to name it after him.

That day, they disembarked at a bay called Buen Suceso, after one of their vessels, and there they met Haush natives[16]. They continued along the waters of the South Atlantic Ocean, exploring the area, studying the shores and the geography of Tierra del Fuego. After nine months of exploring those vast southern seas, they returned to Lisbon.

From that expedition by the Nodal brothers we now treasure some of their names on the maps, such as San Diego Cape, Buen Suceso Bay and Valentín Bay[17]. Nevertheless, the Strait of Le Maire and Cape Horn maintained their names, for at the time, the huge success of the Dutch in terms of discoveries was indisputable.

Buen Suceso Bay is not only important from a historical point of view because of the events I just mentioned, but also because the Coast Guard moved there from Ushuaia in 1887, and operated from there until 1896. Its Commander, Luis Fique, moved there together with his whole family to take over the official outpost.

---

16. They disembarked at the bay on January 23rd, 1619. That was the first contact between Europeans and members of the Haush tribe.

17. San Diego Cape was named after the expedition cosmographer, Diego Ramírez de Arellano; Valentín Bay was named after the pilot of one of the vessels, Valentín Jansen.

Due to all those important events, the bay was declared a National Historic Site by the President of Argentina in 1984[18].

Leaving history aside, I will introduce a few anecdotes here, more related to the trivialities of everyday life. And I say this because being at the Navy outpost was like being at home. They treated us so well and trusted us to such a degree, that it was impossible not to feel at ease. Our stay there was like a small retreat during which we forgot our immediate worries. For a few days, the words walk, cold and distance disappeared from our everyday vocabulary; it was like a temporary amnesia that made us forget about our responsibilities as an expedition. We spent time having fun, playing all sorts of games and watching lots of movies.

The relaxed atmosphere and the beauty of the landscape around the outpost inspired me to write on my diary. I let my mind wander and my pen flow free and unrestricted.

We were lucky enough to see the contour of Staten Island[19]. We were over thirty kilometres away from there but we could still feel its magic. I stayed there for a while, feeding my imagination, building a new world related to that mythical island and all its stories. I thought a lot about Luis Piedrabuena[20], a sailor who was closely connected with that island. And while I am at it, I need to tell you about the time this heroic Argentinean on his schooner *Espora* became wrecked on the shores of that island. I admire his ability, strength and intelligence. With the wreckage of the ship, he built a small vessel, a cutter which he named *Luisito* and aboard which he could safely return to Tierra del Fuego.

I also remembered that on that island there was once a military prison, and I immediately thought about the lighthouse

---

18. Declared National Historic Site by Decree number 3806.

19. The name of Staten Island is connected with the nationality of its discoverers, Le Maire and Shouten, who named it after their homeland: Staten-Generaal of Holland.

20. Argentina granted Staten Island to Luis Piedrabuena in recognition of his work as a rescue worker on the southern seas. He later gave it back to his country, in an act of patriotism. He is thought to have saved the lives of over one hundred shipwrecked people.

located on San Juan del Salvamento, known worldwide as Jules Verne's inspiration for his famous novel *The Lighthouse at the End of the World.*

On that very same spot where I was standing, I made a personal promise to go and visit that island some day. The landscape was visually impressive: the emblematic shape with its pointed peaks covered with a mysterious mist. I am sure that I will never forget that image.

I have not told you about the specific purposes of Buen Suceso outpost yet. One of the reasons why it is there is an act of sovereignty. Another purpose is to control the Strait of Le Maire. A great number of vessels of all flags and with various destinations like Ushuaia, Antarctica, Navarino Island, the Beagle Channel and Cape Horn go through it. Its third and last goal is to transmit the weather forecast to the other bases located in Tierra del Fuego.

After a hearty meal and some after-dinner conversation filled with anecdotes, laughs and movies, I went to bed.

DAY 24 That was the last day we spent at Buen Suceso Bay. We used it to organize the food, get the gear ready and pack our bags. We were back to carrying our home on our backs, like snails. We had a nice meal and we indulged ourselves with the last treats before going back to our lonesome journey. We also spent time examining maps, observing the relief and establishing important points for our journey.

They gave us the visit log book. I was not surprised to see the always cheerful words of Ángel de Andrés and his students. But, for the first time, I found the writings of my personal friend Sergio Anselmino. He conveyed the joy he felt when he got there, but between the lines I could see that he felt sad and lonely. We wrote our experiences down; in a few lines, I described how our mood had changed radically before reaching the outpost, once we reached the bay and, of course, our eternal gratitude to the people at the outpost.

One of the things that they do at Buen Suceso outpost is talk on the radio with Parry outpost, which is located on the neighboring Staten Island. I guess that besides being a nice way to make time go by faster, it helps them feel less isolated, especially the people at Parry, who do not even get to see ships.

As on any other night in the life of those isolated military men, both outposts transmitted over the Strait of Le Maire and the radio frequencies made those two Argentinean units virtually come together. This time, the representatives of Buen Suceso Bay had a great piece of news to share with the people at Parry: three young men were visiting their outpost. I am sure that the people on the other side of the strait wondered how they had got there. Not on boat, plane or helicopter, but walking.

Taking into account they hardly get the chance to talk to anyone at all, it came as no surprise that the people at Parry wanted to speak with those three madmen who had walked over three hundred kilometres and were still planning to walk another two hundred. Of course, we accepted the invitation and talked to them, for it was an honor to be able to exchange ideas and information with them. They gave us their support in our adventure. Just like the people at Buen Suceso Bay, they stay there for forty five days, until the next guard arrives on board the *Alférez Sobral.*

We truly enjoyed our last meal there. After that, we would eat soup, vegetable stock and pasta with no sauce. We were giving up the delicacies of the bourgeoisie to go back to the simple diet of the hiker. I am not complaining about it, it was our choice. We spent the last hours before going to bed playing cards and watching movies.

6
TheFinalStage

From Buen Suceso Bay to Estancia María Luisa

Cowardice is not part of those who are born
sailors or travellers on new lands.

FRANCISCO PASCACIO MORENO

DAY 25 On such a day as this, a 25th of May, Buenos Aires witnessed the onset of a revolution. The situation at the City Hall was difficult; people gathered outside with excitement and filled every corner of the then called Plaza de la Victoria, currently Plaza de Mayo. The people of Argentina wanted to know what was going to happen…

One hundred and ninety-five years elapsed since that May Revolution, which was not an attempt to achieve independence; that would only come some six years later, on July 9th, 1816. To commemorate such an important event in Argentinean history, we took some pictures where we showed the flag.

We were getting ready to leave Buen Suceso Bay. I do not think that we were fully able to put our appreciation for the members of the crew into words to convey how important our stay in Buen Suceso had been to us. We said goodbye to each one of them and departed.

For ten minutes, we enjoyed the infinite pleasure of walking in dry boots. But shortly after, we had to cross a small stream, which put a definite end to the pleasure of dry-feet. The freezing water made me come back to reality, a wilder reality far removed from the comfort of a house, a reality with wet feet and cold bodies.

The tide was low at the time, so we could walk around the Buen Suceso Bay. It was the only time in which that was possible. We did not have a lot of room to move around because just a few metres from the shore there was a very steep hill with thick vegetation. The ground was not the best one to walk on either; there were many big and wet stones. We had to be careful, think over every step before taking it, for the surface was very slippery.

After leaving the outpost, we started moving in a different direction, instead of moving east as we had done for the past twenty-two days, we headed north, and after Cape San Diego, we would walk northwest. Although this might seem irrelevant, it actually had great significance to us for we were, from that moment onward, homeward bound.

None of us said anything, but we were not in a great mood for walking. I could feel it in the air; we all exude a strange feeling. There was no doubt that we were still attached to the comforts and lack of activity of Buen Suceso Bay. But we had to get past it, for it was now part of our increasingly long memory lane, a distant image that faded with the speed of words spoken into the wind.

Once again the time called for moving onward without looking back, to blend with the terrain and adapt ourselves to its varying shapes. Along the coast we found lots of algae, which sometimes even covered the whole area we had, or should have had, for walking. Stepping on them was like trying to dance on a soaped dance floor.

The rocks kept getting bigger and bigger, until we were forced to climb them to continue on our way. When we had the chance, we left the beach and went up the hill. It was easier and faster there. At noon, we stopped to have a luxurious lunch which consisted in *tortas fritas* with *dulce de leche*, the Argentinean milk jam. Like three sybarites, we dove into an unrestricted ocean of gastronomic pleasures - an unprecedented event in the history of the 'Nomads in Mitre'.

We crossed woods and coves, small bends where the salty water sits still. After six hours, we got to San Mauricio Cove.

About its name I can tell you that the cove was discovered by Le Maire and Shouten who named it after Mauricio de Nassau, prince of Holland at the time. I am not sure if the 'saint' that appears before the name of the European noble (God only knows why they added it) was put there following his wishes or not. The truth is that Mauricio has been immortalized as a saint.

Following our traditional tasks, Leo and Juan set up the tent while I tried to light a fire. They completed their task with no difficulties, but I had to admit that all my efforts to shed some light and warmth onto that night were in vain.

I gave up and went inside the tent.

That night was especially strange, Leo fell in a kind of depression once again and, consequently, he vented it on us. There was no doubt that he missed his family. I do not blame him for that; I just tried to let him be for the time being, let him sort out his inner feelings by himself. After eating some stew, we went to bed.

DAY 26 We got up, like we did every day, to the sound of the alarm clock. With all the patience in the universe, we had breakfast inside our sleeping bags.

We left the cove at about eleven in the morning. Leo was still cross, so we decided to leave him alone for a bit.

At least the ground was far better than the previous terrain for walking. First, we walked on the beach for a while and later on we walked on something that resembled a terrace, devoid of trees, where we found many crossing guanaco trails. As the day went by, we came across many of these funny American camels.

Little by little Leo's mood got better. We decided that we could celebrate the occasion singing some out-of-tune songs. The good thing was that no one would complain about the lousy artistic display; after all, our voices drowned in the icy waves and were carried away by the ever-present wind.

I believe that if Mother Nature could think - I do not believe it does, for it is too wise and does not need to do so - she would have imagined that our chants were prayers asking for the grace of gods, for harvests to be plentiful and for our souls to be healthy. And perhaps She would have been right. After five hours of intense walk we made out the unmistakable shape of Cape San Diego. Our voices joined in a single scream '*Lighthouse!*' Like when we screamed *rancho*, it meant having accomplished a mission, having found a small piece in a five hundred kilometres long puzzle.

San Diego lighthouse has a concrete base and, in its upper part, there is a lamp that, by the looks of it, was probably out of order. We did not have to put up our tent, because we could use the structure as our refuge. On the inner walls we found the testimonies of the usual nomads and those of some people we did not know. We saw writings by Ángel de Andrés and Sergio Anselmino, who wrote that he had left Ushuaia and that, without ever leaving the shore, he had reached cape San Diego, the easternmost end of the Island of Tierra del Fuego. A chill went down my spine when I read that he felt fine but immensely alone.

San Diego lighthouse, easternmost end of Tierra del Fuego.

On one of the walls, we saw the words of another adventurer who dared to test and defy his limitations, to undertake a journey against all odds. His name was Salas. He did not write much, he said nothing about his route, age or reasons; he just said that he was travelling by himself. Those words still echo in my mind: *by himself...* Perhaps that is indeed the only way to feel you are a special being in the world, to get immersed into spatial and temporal nothingness, to give up watches and get lost in magical forests, to brave seas and dare mountains. Now that I have experienced it, I can attest that Mitre Peninsula is, without the slightest shadow of doubt, a perfect scenario to achieve this goal.

There was plenty of dry firewood, so lighting a nice fire was an easy task. It was starting to get dark, and the three of us looked, expectantly, at the lamp of San Diego lighthouse. Any moment now, that powerful light would turn on and cast playful shadows over the ocean, lighting the sailors' paths. I was quite disappointed when the place got pitch-black. There was no doubt now, the lighthouse was indeed out of order. There were no lights or ships, just us and a fire that cast some rays of light on our faces.

For dinner, we decided to eat with no restrictions or limitations. We cooked burgers; we had seven each. And we ate them sandwich-style, using some *tortas fritas* that we had left from Buen Suceso Bay. We washed down the food with some tasty *mate*, and some tea. Like on many other nights, it started to rain at the exact moment when we were relaxing, under the warm glow of the fire. I felt the rain come down to tell us to stop, to curb our enjoyment. We went inside the lighthouse and turned in.

DAY 27 Leo's behavior that morning was not what we would have wanted. While Juan and I got everything ready to go, Leo slept in. We had already had breakfast, but he got back in his sleeping bag. We woke him up but he seemed to be buried there, stuck for ever inside that old and useless lighthouse. We encouraged him to get up, for it was getting rather late. My best guess was that he was under the hard grip of homesickness once again, and the only solution to that was the love of his family.

It was an amazing day, not a single cloud around, and the sun shone freely on every corner of the island. To the south of where we were we could clearly see the shape of the unmistakable Atocha, Campana y Pirámide mountains, as well as the Negros mountains. Both sets of mountains meant different things to us. The first range conveyed trust, certainty and joy; around them we had known where to go when we left the coast and we got excellent results. On the other hand, the second range meant uncertainty, weakness and disappointment; being there we had got lost and wandered for about three days. Despite the meanings associated with each set of mountains, they looked especially beautiful. It was odd to think that only ten days ago we were there but on the other side... The Spanish poet Antonio Machado was right when he wrote his famous verses: 'wanderer, there is no road, the road is made by walking.'

The terrain here offered a perfect grip and support for walking. The guanaco trails were very well defined on the hill. We even saw one behind a small hill, but when it saw us just a few metres away, it tried to dash out of sight immediately. It was in such a hurry that it tripped and fell to the ground. It was very funny to see it get up; it looked as if it was being tickled on the ground, for it moved its legs like a person who cannot contain his laughter. It got up in no time, and vanished like a gust of wind. That was a good example of guanaco philosophy, laughing at your own misfortune.

After two hours of difficult walking, we sighted Thetis Bay[1], which seemed to be never-ending. We made a well-deserved stop and ate some *tortas fritas* with cheese. Slowly, we descended towards the coast, from where we could clearly see the geography of the bay. It became narrow in two different spots, like a big bag that you tie in two different places. Right in front of us, on the other side of where the water entered (its width was no greater than thirty metres), there was a set of small houses. We knew there was a way to get to the other side, but we did not know its exact location, it could be in the first or second narrow point. We decided to walk further south following the shore. We crossed a river there, where the water level reached our waist. There was one more to go; the flow was faster and it was not especially narrow. Leo volunteered to give it a go. He took his backpack off, we tied him down with a rope and he started to walk, slowly, towards the opposite bank. He gave up when the water reached his chest. Its flow was strong, and it was hard to walk in it. Clearly, that was not the right place to cross. We had to turn back, and go round the whole bay. But we were not going to do it that day; we would have enough time to cross on the next day.

At a distance, on our side of the bay, we saw a refuge. We thought that it was a good idea to spend the night there. We might even get lucky and find some food there. Leo got there first and just stood in front of the door without going in. Juan and I wondered what treasure our friend had found to be left so awestruck. When we got there we realized that what had caught Leo's attention was a great big hole on the wall opposite the door (that was not even in its place, it was just lying on the ground). Sometimes it is good to look on the bright side of things; life is not as harsh in that way. Should I have just

---

1. Previously named Verschoor after the Rear Admiral of the fleet in the Dutch expedition that Jacques Le Hermite started on April 29th, 1623. The current name was given by the English expedition commanded by Captain Robert Fitz-Roy in memory of the schooner named after the Greek goddess of the sea, daughter of Zeus and Hera, and which was wrecked (supposedly with treasures still inside) at Cape Frio, near Rio de Janeiro in 1830.

taken the immediate reality of what we encountered at face value, I would have said that we got to a run-down refuge, bombarded by invisible pilots determined to extinguish walkers from the face of the earth. But it was nicer to say that we found a nice bright room with a view to the ocean.

Once again, we proved ourselves that we were a united, fast and effective team. While I lit the fire, Leo and Juan looked around for wood, tidied our stuff and baked *tortas fritas*. That is the way it works in a team, many different members doing their share. After a few minutes, we were relaxing, enjoying some *mates* and some freshly baked *tortas fritas*. There was nothing else we wanted at the moment; we had food, warm clothes and a place to sleep. We had the essentials covered and had no need for a car, a house, money or investments. We just needed air, fire, water and earth, the four basic survival elements.

Although the refuge had a big hole in it, it seemed like the wind chose the door to step inside. Leo and Juan put their strength and creativity to work and managed to put the door back in place. Using a piece of plastic that we had to put underneath the tent, they built a sort of barrier that they put over the door frame before putting the door in place. It was a great work of art, perhaps the nicest and most useful in the whole peninsula. That system worked so well that we called that refuge the 'Refuge with the Airtight Door.'

We cooked a bean and rice stew. We had dry clothes, we had a full belly and we were happy. By the warmth of the fire, we were never short of things to talk about. We spoke about our personal desires, our ideas and points of view. It was funny to think about what we would do when we came back to that which people call civilization. Food was never left out of the conversation, and among the things that we would eat upon returning, *dulce de leche, alfajores* (a kind of sweet pastry made up by two cookies stuck together with a sweet filling), ice-cream, beef, and mashed potatoes and vegetables made the top six. We actually would eat anything prepared by the loving hands of a nice woman, a caring mother or a pampering granny.

Leo estimated that it would take us another five days to get to Estancia María Luisa. I was a little more cautious and guessed that it would take us a little under a week to reach our final destination.

After picking up some wood for the fire and drinking a tasty tea, I went to bed.

DAY 28 When I woke up I saw some rays of light coming in through the many holes in the refuge. I could not see clearly from where I was at the moment, but I guessed that it was a beautiful day for walking.

After reorganizing everything and replenishing the wood at the refuge, we started to walk. I was right; although it was still a bit cold, the sky was clear and the sun shone unrestrained. I remembered the words that Sergio Anselmino had said about going round Thetis Bay; now it was our turn to do it. According to what he said, it would take us about six hours. The only difference was that Sergio had walked during the night, so I thought that perhaps it would take us fewer hours. Out of all his description, what I remembered most was that the lonesome walker had revealed to us the existence of small streams along the way. But they were not like those that we call streams; because they were not wide, but they were deep and their water was blackish. I can attest to that because an hour after departing, I crossed one and the water reached my stomach. These little rivers extended far beyond our line of sight - therefore we had no choice but to face them and so, we plunged into their mysterious depths. There is no point in saying that we were not cold, for we were, but walking at a steady pace helped warm up our bodies. I imagined that the day would be plentiful in those crossings, but luckily we only had to cross two more. But even that was more than enough.

At about noon, we ate some *tortas fritas* that Leo had prepared the previous day. I remember that he was complaining that they had come out a little rubbery. As far as I am concerned, those were the best *tortas fritas* I have ever had. Perhaps I thought so because I was terribly hungry, but I believe they were truly delicious.

We had moved forward at a nice and steady pace for two hours. Looking at the map, we concluded that we could not be too far from the other side of the bay, from the earthly paradise where we would find the ultimate glory of sleeping in a refuge. It was low tide again, so that simplified our progress. We got to a place where the ground was soft; certainly we were walking on land that remained underwater during high tide. At that point, we crossed a river and were very happy to be on the other side, as it was firmer ground there. We videotaped the moment; Juan got us on camera when we got to the other side. We jumped up and down and cheered out of joy, because we were closer to that day's destination. We walked for another half hour and we got to the refuges that we expected to find, those that we had seen and craved for the previous day from a hill on the other side of the bay. The first structures that we found had been part of the outpost of the Argentinean Coast Guard which was there from 1889 until 1895, and a house where the brave men who settled there to work in a sea lion tannery had lived. They did not look that bad on the outside, but inside they were in bad shape. There were pots, empty bottles and a stove that no longer work because it was absolutely rusted. Next to the structures there was an old steam boiler where they must have boiled sea lion fat. We kept on walking and we found a plaque placed there by the Salesian mission in memory of Monsignor Fagnano when he came to these lands. He had been the chaplain of an expedition lead by Ramón Lista, which started on October 31st, 1886. Polidoro Segers, who acted as doctor, was also part of that exploration trip, together with 25 other men[2].

A few metres further down, we found what would become our sanctuary for the night. There was a sign on top of the door that read: Refuge. We could not think of a better word for that moment. After such a long walk, we wanted to rest. Leo was walking a little bit behind us, so we tried to play a joke on him and told him that the refuge was nothing but an old run-down tin structure. He did not fall for it. It was one of the

---

2. Lista's expedition was commissioned by the national government and had the main mission of carrying out a topohydrographic, anthropological and linguistic study of the shores between San Sebastián Bay and Thetis Bay. It was the first time that Argentineans travelled that route, so it was an important geopolitical consolidation mission. During that expedition there was a terrible fight between Ramón Lista's troops and the Selk'nams in the bay of San Sebastián, with a result of twenty-six dead natives.

best refuges that we found; it had some tables, plenty of chairs, beds almost in perfect shape and a salamander stove that was a lot better than what we had imagined. Actually, it was not a salamander stove but a metal container and it was in good condition because Sergio Anselmino had replaced it the year before. I have seen pictures of the old one and I think Sergio should be commended for his generosity. The place was so clean that it surpassed the standards of the real estate properties that we had found in the peninsula.

On one of the walls, there was quite a sizeable larder. Before opening it, I imagined that we would find all kinds of food treasures inside, but out of the few things that were there, we rescued some dried basil, a flavor that was absolutely foreign to us at the time and which was highly appreciated. I felt like those sailors of days gone by, who after sailing the immensities of the ocean for very long days came to some island rich in spices. Of course, we did not find tons of basil, but it was more than enough to season our foods. Besides, we did not have the need to feed an entire kingdom.

Everywhere inside the refuge we could read the words written by those who had visited the place before us. Some just wrote their name; others detailed their journey, dates, reasons and even feelings. And since I am speaking about them, I should mention the log book. The people who wrote there did so at their leisure, with no hurry, telling every detail about their trip: Ángel de Andres and his students, Osvaldo Bianchi, Sergio Anselmino. I remember that Sergio spoke extensively about his lonesome journey, but not with the coldness of a chronicler, but with the spontaneous warmth of a son. In his words he thanked his mother and showed tokens of the love he felt for her. Another entry that also touched me deeply was that by Adolfo Imbert. He spoke at length about the importance of horses and about how noble they were as animals and as means of transport. Despite all technological advances, steeds would always be a key element in the life of men. I totally agree. One of the expeditions that he described included the names of all its members, both human and equine. Don

Quixote would not have been the same without its horse, Rocinante. Perhaps in the same line of thought, some bikers wrote down their names next to the cubic capacity of their machines. That testimony shocked me somehow: I think I would feel the same if I found a farmer in an outpost using a computer. Besides, engines do not have a soul, so they are not worthy of being mentioned.

We went out with Juan to look for firewood, and we were surprised to see a dog, almost as black as night itself, jump into a river that was near the refuge. We did not know where that animal had come from. We knew about him as little as he knew about us. The only thing we knew is that it was there, and then he fled and vanished into thin air. We never saw him again. There was no one there, so I am sure that it was a wild dog.

Some metres behind the refuge, we found some old structures that certainly dated back to when the sea lion tannery had worked there over half a century ago, from 1946 to 1952 and that belonged to the SADICCAP Corporation (Argentinean Society for the Industry, Trade, Hunting and Fishing). They

Old Coast Guard building and a seal tannery. Thetis Bay.

exploited sea lions both for their fur and their fat. The latter was used to supply the tannery and to lubricate the heavy machinery. But in order to do that, they first had to turn fat into oil. At the same time, the fur had low market value in comparison with furs from South Africa, Uruguay and Alaska. As living proof of that competitive disadvantage against other markets, there are thousands of abandoned furs. They are just piled up there, like an open door cemetery, a monument that like many others speaks of men's greed and stupidity. Surely the bright minds that founded the company never even considered the possibility of the freight and labor being actually higher than the revenues generated by the furs.

Many of the sea lions that were slaughtered on Thetis Bay were herded all the way from Cape San Vicente, located to the northwest of the bay. For the sea lions not to go into the sea they had to be surrounded. Many times the slaughterers had a hard time when facing female sea lions with their offspring, as they become more aggressive during that period.

We came back to our luxurious refuge. When we went in, we were pleased to see the playful sparkles already dancing in the air. But I think that the best of it all was to see Leo immediately starting to bake some *tortas fritas*. Once cooked, we ate some with cheese and pâté de foie. They tasted great.

It was my turn to later on cook some dinner – pasta with ragout sauce. Luckily, we had some tomato puree boxes left that we had brought from the outpost at Buen Suceso Bay.

After a very long after-dinner conversation, I made an entry in my diary. There were many things to be told, events that could not be left out of that book which I would perhaps read in my golden years, pages that perhaps would help me come back, at least with my mind, to this dreamlike place, to this magical area called Mitre Peninsula.

By the candle light, we started reading the log book in more detail. Page after page we read the words of those anonymous heroes that had been there at some point in time, heroes who were known nowhere but here, as if they were characters in a story with no defined identity - timeless experiences, ephemeral achievements. The Mitre Peninsula is like that: a place that inspires and mesmerizes; that seduces you and takes you far beyond your own limitations. You discover your hidden abilities, invisible powers, and mighty strengths. In Mitre, there are no watches, time is infinite; dawns are eternal; nights are unbreakable. Each being and each landscape has its own place under the sun. Everything is predefined, in perfect balance. It is an island inside an island, a piece of the territory that is unlike the rest of Tierra del Fuego.

There were only two beds, and as Leo was the biggest one of the three, Juan and I had to share a bunk.

DAY 29 We got up, had breakfast and got ready to start walking. We left the refuge in better conditions than it was in when we got there, signed the log book and left.

At quarter past eleven we were on the trail. If someone had seen us, they would have thought that we were three merchants who were carrying valuable objects to trade at distant towns lost beyond the horizon, hidden behind a desert tainted with abandonment. But our reality was different; we did not want to trade anything or make any money, we were just three men who had decided to challenge themselves.

Shortly after, we made the first stop at the 'Tres Amigos' (three friends) outpost. At least that is what the map said. We ate the last *tortas fritas* with some pâté and drank some tea. Like other travellers had done before us, we left our signature on the refuge walls: 'Nomads in Mitre' had *tortas fritas* for lunch here. May 29th, 2005.'

As we moved forward, we found one valley after the other. It was very tiresome to go up and down all the time, but there was no other choice. At least we had no problems walking, because we did not have to cross through woods and the ground was firm. At a given moment, six condors, owners of the sky and the mountains, flew up from the depths of the valley and started to fly toward us, putting up a private show for us, drawing abstract shapes up in the air. Once again the circumstances made us feel privileged.

From the opposite valley, Leo realized that he had left his walking pole in the previous one, surely where we had stopped to take some pictures. We would have liked to have the strength and will to go back and get it, but Leo decided to leave it there. It must still be there, bearing heavy winds, cold rain and sunlight. I am sure that whoever finds it, will take it as proof that someone was there before, another ghost that prevailed over the vast terrain, as evidence of an unknown knight who fought against oblivion.

But our most pleasant surprise was when, after climbing a hill, the condors started to emerge one by one, until twenty of them where flying together over us. Believe it or not, that is true, twenty condors in the sky! Watching closely over us, twenty condors going up and down with their gigantic spread-out wings, with their white collars and their beaks and crests; twenty condors that seemed to represent Mother Nature's perfect harmony.

I do not know for how long that show went on; I was engulfed in the enjoyment and lost track of time. The watch either stopped ticking or ran faster. The fact is that those birds playing through the clouds were a representation of something out of the ordinary, something beyond everyday experiences. It was something different, which cannot and should not be measured in seconds, minutes or hours.

While I was taking some pictures of the show, I saw a cow getting near me, looking at me with a mad look in its eyes. Obviously, I was in its way, so I reacted by moving to give it enough room to go by. We understood each other well, the cow went her way and I went mine. I learnt later on that Leo and Juan saw the whole scene from a little distance away, and found it rather amusing.

We had to go on, we still had some kilometres to walk; we had to stash those landscapes somewhere in our memories and keep on moving forward.

We reached Centenario Cove. We exited the hilly area and walked towards the estuary. Quite a lot of water ran in its course, and watching it flow into the ocean was like watching two armies fighting over a piece of land. The cove went some kilometres further south, but I was sure that we had to go all the way round it to cross to the other side.

It was the safest bet. Once we started walking, Leo and Juan thought that it was worth it to try and cross close to the estuary. I was certain that it was madness to try, but I accepted anyway and went back to the starting point. When we got there I told them: 'Ok, there it is, cross it. I'll wait for you here'. So I waited, watching the water flow; I waited for them to make up their minds, pondering whether they would risk their lives crossing a river that would surely drag them to their death, and all to save a couple of kilometres. Eventually they came to their senses and understood, as I had, that going round was the sensible choice. The important thing is to realize that there is always a way back, no matter what decision you have made, you can go back and mend your mistakes. So there we were, retracing our steps, walking up that cove, going round its banks. After half an hour, we found a place that seemed suitable for crossing. So we crossed with the water barely over our knees. Once on the other side, we encountered a silver fox that ran away as soon as it set eyes on us. Perhaps it was the first time that it had seen a human being.

It was already five in the afternoon, the sun was setting and the sky was getting grayish with black patches. We did not want to stop; we wanted to get to Estancia Policarpo that day. There was still a long way to go; it was madness, but something beyond reason made us keep moving, stepping into that anonymous night, defying time and walking in unknown territory, trusting nothing but our senses for orientation. We let instinct, perceptions, the sounds of nature and the textures of the ground guide us. Little by little, we managed to merge with the landscape, the terrain, and we became an active part of the Mitre Peninsula.

We walked for a long time on the wide sandy beach flanked by steep cliffs; we could hardly see them, but they were there, right by our side. Alone amidst such landscapes, in that desert full of ghosts, three wanderers illuminated by the power of their souls. After travelling for endless kilometres, and after revisiting the sources of forgotten stories, we reached the place that we were looking for. Juan confirmed this by shouting 'cove' with all his might. Leo and I also started shouting that word of triumph that only we could hear and that, somehow, made us feel closer to civilization. We were sure that we were on the coast of Falsa Cove, the same place where, in 1767, the vessel *Purísima Concepción* was wrecked. The same cove that had sheltered its shipwrecked sailors, those men who had celebrated the first mass in Tierra del Fuego, those who, after months of hard work, could build a boat that would take them safely back to the city of Buenos Aires. Two hundred and thirty eight years had elapsed since that episode, since such an important event for Tierra del Fuego. We were there, two centuries later, on a Sunday night in the autumn of 2005. And even then, after such a long time, their ghosts, the legends of distant days, still walked on freely almost right through us.

The ocean was close; we had to walk on the big rocks whose surface was flat and slippery, wet from the endless battering of the ocean waves. We tripped, we fell, but we always got up again. We hurt our hands, our feet, our knees, but despite everything, our hearts kept on beating and warming our bodies. We kept on moving and at a given point in time we decided to use our flashlight, the only one we had left – our 'firefly'. While we walked, it beamed narrow, intermittent rays of lights, small patches of brightness that did not suffice to light up that black night.

We could not find the estancia, it was already late, and we did not have a clear idea of where we were exactly. Leo and Juan swore that they saw something, a vague shape, an undefined silhouette, somewhere in the distance. The miracle happened shortly after crossing a narrow stream. Right next to us, my flashlight showed us parts of it. Yes, we had found a refuge. Our traditional celebrations were louder than ever. If we had had something to drink besides the black peat water, like wine or cider, we would have toasted the moment. Despite our joy, I was a little disappointed with the run-down state in which we found our home for the night. It had no windows, there were holes in the walls; it suffered from the signs of the passing of time, and some inconsiderate people. Juan and I set out on a last minute mission, to look for another refuge. It could not be; there had to be something decent around; Estancia Policarpo had been quite important in its prime. We walked for a while on muddy soil and, eventually, found a refuge that to us, was a lot more than just a hut; it could have been the magnificent residence of a great wool baron, a powerful lord who had left his mark in that part of Tierra del Fuego. This called for a second celebration; the 'facilities', as we used to call the things we found in the refuges (general conditions, cleanliness, salamander stove, etc.) were above standard. There were some mattresses; the salamander stove was in perfect condition; and there was even a larder with some food in it. The pearl in that small treasure chest was, beyond any doubt, a can of tomato sauce. We also found other less valuable things like coffee bags, sugar and a pack of *yerba* for *mate* of a brand that we had never heard of. Perhaps it was exclusively distributed there in the Mitre Peninsula... We went back to inform Leo of our finding and, right away, we gathered firewood to warm our castle. The place heated up quite fast, and we could take our coats off. We celebrated the successful day by eating some pasta with sauce. That was indeed gourmet food, not to mention the coffee with lots of sugar (real sugar, no sweeteners), that we drank after dinner. It was nine in the evening; we were relaxed and happy. It had been a tough day, we had walked for ten hours at a steady pace, but, luckily, we were already there, by the heat of the stove, drinking coffee and chatting about life. About that day, I wrote the following on my journal:

'Things could not have gone better. I prayed to God intensely for him to guide us in the darkness of the night. At moments I was afraid, but luckily we had the courage, the strength and the hope to keep on going. Once again I feel (and I am almost sure that this is the case) that there is a higher being who wants us to be successful. I am very grateful for that, and I am more than happy with my two expedition partners and friends. I think we make a good team. We are closer to our goal. I already feel that I will miss this nomadic life.'

DAY 30 We opened our eyes to a glorious morning; it was ten. The refuge was blissfully flooded by the mighty sunlight determined to snatch us from our dreams, letting us know that we should go out and enjoy the beautiful day.

After drinking a tasty cup of coffee, I decided that I had to give fishing another go. I grabbed an old can with a line that I found outside the house and headed for the coast. On my way, I found some abandoned structures, bent by the invisible forces of the passing of time. It is worth mentioning that Policarpo was once upon a time a great estancia. Their main activity was sheep shearing. Between 1965 and 1966, they reached a production level of one hundred and sixty wool bales, which meant a total of 35,227 kilograms of wool[3]. The vessels that reached Falsa Cove had the double purpose of bringing supplies and fetching bales. Some years later, due to a significant mange outbreak, the owners of Estancia Policarpo decided to turn to cattle raising.

Coming back to our own story, the house that looked like the most important of all the buildings there was absolutely run-down, crushed. The only structure that was still standing was a press that once had been used to press wool.

Because of that estancia, because of the wreck of the *Purísima Concepción* vessel, and the fact that it hosted the first mass of Tierra del Fuego, Falsa Cove is today a National Historical Site[4].

When I got to the shoreline I stopped thinking about history and adventurers of days gone by. I decided to empty my mind and focus on the art of fishing. I just wanted to concentrate so that a fish would bite on the hook that I cast over and over again. After trying all possible spots, of casting harder, further, slower, I finally run out of patience and accepted that I would go back empty-handed once again. Clearly, fishing was not my thing.

---

3. Data from Francisco Bilbao's personal letters currently held at the Records of the Museo del Fin del Mundo.

4. Declared National Historical Site by Decree number 64, 1999.

Some people say it is all about luck, but I believe saying that is belittling this art; there is a lot of skill involved in it, mastered by those who are good at it.

I went back thinking that you should never lose hope. Besides, it was already noon and I started to feel hungry.

When I got to the refuge, I caught Leo and Juan eating some pasta with basil. I could only eat a little that was left. Once again, I had to hear Leo and Juan make fun of my poor fishing skills, which by now had become a standing joke. They told me that if the expedition had depended on me as the source of food, we would have surely starved to death. We had rice for seconds, which was quite tasty.

After lunch, Leo read to us some lines that he had written down. He spoke about his wife and kids, and of how much he loved them and missed them. He could not hold his feelings in and broke down in tears. By then, our souls were more emotional; our hearts were open wide. We had shared lots of things by then, long days; a whole month had gone by since we had left Ushuaia. Thirty days without seeing his loved ones was sufficient explanation for those tears rolling down from Leo's sad eyes.

Juan also shared with us some words that he wrote down in the log book of the refuge. It was with great sorrow that he spoke about how much he loved his brothers, his parents and his girlfriend. He cried calmly and deeply, letting his tears flow together with his words. I did not want to cry, I think I had the simple belief that if I let myself be moved, it would be negative for me. Perhaps it is for that reason that I tried to avoid thinking about how much I missed my people, about the infinite love that I felt for them. Or at least I made an effort not to show that in the lines I wrote in my diary, currently my aid for writing this book. We hugged each other firmly; sometimes we just needed to feel loved, to support each other. We were a team, and as such, we needed that bond and we needed to understand each other. And in that sense I have no complaints; quite the opposite, I think that we made good use of it. We were always there for the team, which is essential for living together for thirty six days, especially in the context of such an expedition.

At four in the afternoon, we started walking, once again on the road, putting distance between the present and the past. That was our trip; we could not stay at a single place longer than strictly necessary, just enough time to record it onto our memories. The shape of Bilbao Peak started to disappear from the horizon as we moved closer to the Atlantic shore. We saw hundreds of cows running freely on those desolate lands, going into the forest and out of sight. From the main house, we started to see the trails of quadbikes, and next to them rubbish, signs of recklessness, traces of civilization. The Atlantic coast of the peninsula is easily accessed on motorbikes. Most of the people that go there do so during the summertime.

At about six, we saw Policarpo Cove. The sun was already setting, and the sky had those marvellous shades of red, orange and yellow. Now that I mention it, I think that perhaps history got it wrong, perhaps Magellan and his crew called this part of the world the 'Land of Fire' not because of the bonfires lit by the natives on the shore, but for dusks such as this one, where the whole sky seemed to be on fire.

I tried to cross the cove near its estuary. It was impossible, just like the previous day; the water was running too fast.

I gave up when I felt the cold water slap my chest, and decided to return before the river took me to a sure death. We decided to do the same thing we had done with Centenario Cove, and started walking upstream. We walked slowly for over an hour on soft and wet soil where it was easy to sink in the mud and sand. During high tide, the waters covered the areas where we were now walking. Luckily for us, the cove was draining its water then, so the level of the river was at its lowest.

It was almost dark now and we kept looking desperately for a crossing point. Without giving it much thought, we started crossing the Policarpo River towards the other bank. I was scared; we could hardly see a thing. I remember that moment: we were walking in a line. It was awful not to know how much longer we had to go to reach the other side and to see nothing but dark water. The water never went past our knees, and it was a great relief to reach the other shore; we had been successful in crossing but we had run a great risk, we had been reckless, and we felt the weight of the decision. We hugged tightly and, in tears, Leo asked for us not to run those unnecessary risks ever again.

The place was completely clear; there were just a couple of bushes. We decided not to light a fire and save our energy for the next day. We cooked some pasta with tuna under the apse. We washed it down with tea and coffee. We agreed that crossing the Policarpo River in complete darkness had been plain dumb. I think we unconsciously felt that time was starting to put pressure on us, to force us to be hasty when we should be calm. Wanting to get there faster, we ran the risk of never actually getting there…

As I did every night, I wrote a few lines before going to bed.

DAY 31   It was a very cold morning. Putting on wet socks, underpants, trousers and boots was a true torture. Once dressed, we put the tent down and finished organizing our packs. It was hard to warm up, but we finally did it. The ground was really wet. It was very funny when Juan tried to cross what seemed to be a stream at first sight. He crossed it like he was going to get only his ankles wet. He got a little surprised when he felt the water all the way up his chest. Poor Juan, it was early and cold, but at least it was sunny. Of course he did not find it funny, but Leo and I laughed out loud and played jokes on him.

The shore was a lot further than I had imagined. Just before reaching it, we found some wild horses. They were running free next to one another; there were more than ten, and their long manes fluttered as a sign of freedom, like the image of freedom that most people have. They were all beautiful; it seemed like they had been picked by the best breeders to match the fascinating landscape.

At a distance, we saw what should have been the old refuge Donata. It was not worth it to go there; it was far away and they had told us that it was absolutely run-down. Once we reached the coast, we found parts of the wrecked *Duchess of Albany*[5]. If there ever was a symbol with which I identified the Mitre Peninsula, it was that ship. I had seen pictures of the ship, lying on the beach, heeled over against the solitude of those beaches. Although it was destroyed, those pictures still showed its deck, its spar and several parts that identified it as a ship. It was

---

5. Currently, its figurehead can be seen on the main room of the Museo del Fin del Mundo. '*Figureheads date back a long time, perhaps as long as the first ship that sailed the ocean. Egyptian galleys and Phoenician vessels had their bow covered in art. They represented gods, animals and sometimes women or men who would protect the vessel against the evil sea, its depths and legends. Up to the 17th century, figureheads had a religious or totemic value. By the early 18th century, they became offerings or tributes to important ladies on high society or the nobility. They were mostly carved in wood, showing typical attitudes that were fashionable at the time, mythological symbols or reproductions of human heads emerging from the sea. They represent the ship that named them or gave life to them.*' ZANOLA, Oscar, PEOAF 84, Museo del Fin del Mundo, 1986.

no longer the same; before us we had the remainders of something that would vanish in time, next to those black and white pictures that had dazzled me once and had driven me to live the adventure that we were now completing. That is why I think that I should cast some light on the mystery of this vessel, for when these few parts that remain vanish, there will be nothing left but memories.

It was July 13, 1893. The *Duchess of Albany*, a three masted British sailboat, cruised the Fuegian winter powered by its cold winds. The fog hindered visibility. After months of sailing, having departed from England, bound for Brazil, the ship entered the southern seas – those seas that try to obliterate every trace of humans from their blue, immense, rough waters. With an iron will, the rough men had endured the harsh weather. But they knew that they still had a long journey ahead of them, they still had to go thousands of miles to reach Valparaíso in Chile. At least they were closer, near the shores of Tierra del Fuego. They never imagined that on that morning those lands of legends, that region where the fires lit by the natives illuminated the night at the end of the earth, would exert such an attraction on the vessel, a kind of mysterious spell, that the *Duchess of Albany* would remain forever stranded on those beaches. The British vessel soon started having serious problems. I imagine the captain and crew struggling desperately against their fate, using all their strength and energy to avoid hitting the coastline. But despite all efforts, despite that brave attempt to avoid what would be the end of its final journey, the vessel hit the beach, near Policarpo Cove.

There were no victims; the whole crew managed to disembark. They had to camp near that treacherous coast, for it was already four in the morning. On the next day, twelve of the twenty-eight shipwrecked sailors under the command of the captain, sailed on a boat towards Thetis Bay, where they arrived three days later. From there they were taken by the Coast Guard to Ushuaia on board an Argentine vessel called *Golondrina*. After what had happened the previous day, the rest of the group decided to walk. One of the sixteen sailors joined the natives and stayed with them until his death. The rest of the group, save for one that went missing, was guided by the natives to Thetis Bay, where they were rescued by the ship *Amadeo*, coming from the Chilean city of Punta Arenas. Imagine those sailors walking on freezing winter days, crossing rivers and frozen streams, in pain because of cold, hunger and loneliness.

Some researchers have spoken about this ship as if it was just another ghost sailing the southern seas. Nevertheless, others, like Oscar Zanola[6], have been seduced by its mysteries and have studied its history in depth to discover the true facts.

As to us, we stayed for a while on the beach looking at the ancient vessel while eating some chocolate bars with some coffee and *mate*.

Once back on track, we had to cross yet another river, Luz River. We found the same wild horses that we had seen less than an hour ago. We saw where they crossed the river and we chose a place that was nearby. The water was a little over our waist. We kept walking steadily, without pausing and at a fast pace. We did not find lots of difficulties; it was simple enough to follow the coastline. Besides, we were aided by the local guides: cows and horses that moved forward every time we got near them. They ran away from us and, unknowingly, showed us where to go.

We went near Policarpo Bay, which is actually a big lagoon connected to the sea when the water level is unusually high. We kept walking along the coast until we were forced to go up a hill. From a higher point we saw the Bueno River and the outpost on the opposite bank. It was just a few minutes after five in a glorious afternoon. We saw a bridge that had once crossed the river. Now we only saw half of it there.

Once we got near the river, we decided that we should try crossing it. I volunteered to go first. I tried to cross it near the

---

6. Oscar Zanola was, for many years, the Director of the Museo del Fin del Mundo. He visited the Mitre Peninsula many times, by air or sea. As a researcher he was especially interested in the *Duchess of Albany*. He provided us with valuable information about this shipwreck.

bridge, but I gave up when the water hit my chest. We looked for another spot, nearer the shoreline, right in front of the outpost. But once again, I gave up when it kept getting deeper and deeper. I tried one more time, hundreds of metres downstream. Same results. I started to feel cold. I wanted to warm up a bit, so I walked frantically. Leo and Juan were brewing some hot coffee. On top of feeling cold, I started to lose control, my mind was racing and my feeling and ideas were in turmoil, I could not help thinking the worst things imaginable. We had been there for an hour already. On the opposite bank, there was a boat, motionless, that seemed to laugh at all our failed attempts of crossing to where it was. We thought that we could swim to it and bring it to this side, but we did not know its conditions or if it had oars or holes. We decided not to run the risk. Without second thoughts, we set a time for crossing the river: we would do it at 7 pm. According to our tide cycle chart, the water level should decrease by then. But, unfortunately, it was not so. Everything was just like before, with the exception that now it was darker; a perfect framework for a play where the whole cast was made up by three characters; solitude, the landscape and us. Just before crossing, I asked Leo and Juan what we would do should the river be too deep. There was no answer. In a resolved manner, we walked into the cold waters that got deeper and deeper. We barely noticed that we had lost our footing and that we were adrift, unable to swim because of our heavy backpacks. I panicked; I could no longer see anything, I did not know where the opposite bank was. I remember that I thought I was going to die, that I would never find the way out of that maze that we had created ourselves. Before letting go and surrendering my life, I thought of my parents, my brothers and my friends; I needed to feel them close, to have a mental picture of each and every one of my loved ones. If I ever wanted to see them again, I had to do something, and fast. I decided to let go off my backpack, let the river take it. I could think about nothing but saving my life. I untied the strap that ran across my chest first, and when I was about to take off the one around my waist, a flash of hope struck me from the depths of my soul: I had just felt the ground with the tip of my foot. Leo made it before I did. We called out Juan's name, but we got no answer. It was darker now. Suddenly the moonlight reflected off the cover of Juan's backpack, which was floating in the river. Underneath it, we could see the third musketeer. We reacted immediately and got him out of there. He was alright, but I swear that I feared the worst. He seemed confused, he wanted to go back and get a pole and a glove that he had lost in the crossing.

We checked the refuge. We chose a place where we found two beds, although there were no supplies and the salamander stove had no damper. Leo started crying and the three of us hugged. We had gone through an unpleasant experience, and I can assure you that I had never, ever, been that close to death. Juan was very cold, so I started to get worried. I made him drink the tea that we carried with us in our thermos. We undressed and put on some dry clothes that had survived the crossing because we had put them into waterproof bags. Leo's sleeping bag did get wet though, so the three of us had to share the two dry ones.

In my jacket pocket, I carried the only watch we had, which got wet as well and stopped working for ever. The watch stopped at 7 o'clock, which is the time that we now see as the time of our rebirth. And as it was a group birth, we could say that from that moment onwards we became triplets.

And in order to share with you the real feelings that it had on that night, this is what I wrote:

'It was a frightening experience, an experience that I do not ever want to repeat. God saved us this time, and as we said after the event, we were reborn. But I do not think that we will be so lucky next time, especially if we keep being this reckless. It is a lesson from which we have to learn many things so as not to make this kind of mistake again, under any circumstance. We lived through a tough moment, and we all had a very, very bad time. Nobody said this out loud, but I think that tonight we are somehow in mourning.'

We lit some candles that we found on a shelf that was hanging on one of the walls. There was also a pack of cookies filled with cream. It was not very funny when we opened it and found it empty. As a consolation prize, we ate some crackers we found there that tasted as close to pure dampness as you can get, and some bread that was older than the refuge itself; of course even those treats are highly appreciated in the Mitre Peninsula. I decided to go round the refuge once again. That is how I found a nearby structure that served as meat deposit. I went in and found several pieces of meat hanging from some logs. I went looking for Juan to show him the treasures that I had found. Thinking it was *charqui*, he took a big bite off one piece, like a starving dog. He realized immediately that he was actually eating raw meat, and spit it out onto the ground. I cut one of the pieces in half with an old, rusty saw I found there. The meat was black on the outside, although on the inside there were some red parts that contrasted with the pale green shade of the worms that were enjoying their own banquet. We cut another piece and got the same result, hundreds of spongy vermin feeding from the same meat that we would eat. We only had to choose the really red parts and eliminate those disgusting beings that crawled before our eyes. The rest was simple: 'heat kills everything off,' I said to Leo and Juan over and over again while I fried some meat in lots of fat. In order to mitigate the foul stench of the meat we were about to eat, we added lots of spices to the pot. Despite all those attempts, and even taking into account that we were ravishing, I have no doubts that it was the most disgusting thing I have ever eaten. That is why Leo and I decided to give up on the local food to cook something from our own stash, the one we had been carrying on our backs for over thirty days now. Juan would have kept on eating that disgusting meat, but we forced him to stop. At least eating our food, we ran no risk of food poisoning.

After dinner, we drank some *mate*. We needed to relax, try to forget the unpleasant episode and celebrate the fact of being still alive. But to be honest, we were in no mood for celebrations; we just wanted to hit the sack, try to dream of something beautiful, of relatives and friends, of beings who, on the other side of the world, would be missing us and sending their love and hugs telepathically. We decided to spend the next day on the Bueno River outpost. We still had to dry our clothes, get our gear organized and get ready for the final stage of our adventure, which was coming to an end. Besides, we really needed a day off.

DAY 32 That night was not at all comfortable. We were three people sleeping in a bed for one. The bright side was that we were not cold.

We woke up at ten with the light that entered the room from every window so brightly and intensely that it seemed that the sun itself was right behind those walls.

While Leo and Juan started to fix breakfast, I went outside to explore the surroundings. I was not convinced of the fact that the room we had spent the night in was the only room available, the refuge looked a lot bigger. And I was right; there was a door that led to what seemed the main room in the refuge. Everything was tidy there; there was a stove in perfect condition with hundreds of dry logs, ready to be lit. In the middle of the room there was a table with a jar full of sugar on it. That was the first miracle. Behind me, very close to the entrance, there was a wooden cabinet with four doors. I started fantasizing about the delicacies that I would find inside. I started to open those doors, one by one. In the first one, I found some powder milk and a pack of grated cheese. My heart was already beating faster. The second drawer surprised me with a can of coffee with milk and sugar, which had more than half of its content. I was getting even more excited. The third door was a little of a disappointment, just some spices. When I opened the fourth door my heart skipped a beat altogether. It was as if an army of angels with the whole heavenly court welcomed me with open arms saying: 'Yes, this is a gift for you. This is what you were looking for.' Inside I found a bag with over ten kilos of flour. That was the second miracle. I ran to tell my friends what I had found. They both looked sad; the memories of the river crossing still had a grip on their hearts. They were brewing some tea, so I said to them in an agitated voice: 'I want to drink lots of coffee with lots of milk and sugar, and eat lots of *tortas fritas*...' They both gave me a puzzled look, so they dropped what they were doing and followed me into the other room to see what I'd found with their own eyes. They could not believe it; the bitterness of the previous night had suddenly vanished. And it was absolutely justified; we would spend a whole day eating delicacies, treasures that fate itself had given us to improve our mood. The team started to work once again. Half an hour later, the fire was heating the stove, Leo was kneading the first round of *tortas fritas* and, meanwhile, I cut some wood near the refuge. We hung our wet clothes near the fire to dry them.

There was a smaller room next to the one we were cooking in. There, I found several fishing cans, with lines and hooks; which made me think that the guy who lived there fished quite frequently. I said to myself, why not, perhaps I can do it this time. I got some bait (I used the meat that we had not eaten) and cast four different lines into various spots in the river. Perhaps I would be lucky enough to catch a sea bass or a trout. I had all day long; I was not worried about time. Juan was wearing the farmer's clothes (he had found them at the outpost). He thought that it would be easier for him to catch one of the horses dressed like that. I must admit that he tried very hard, but the stallions remained every inch as free as before. Inside the refuge, our baker kept on kneading *tortas fritas*, which were now piling up on a wooden dish.

We drank *mate* for a long time, while thinking about the previous day. Leo confided in me and told me that he really appreciated me as a friend, and that he especially admired my strong will. I also said I appreciated him as a friend, and in general terms I spoke about how well the team had worked throughout the whole expedition. It was obvious that the river crossing episode had had an impact on us and we were feeling more emotional. We were like three little paper ships that had been completely soaked and left limp, almost destined to founder. We could only live on hope to feed the passion that would lead us to surmount the dangers of the peninsula.

Later on, I went to the river bank to check on the lines that I had cast a while ago. No luck; so I cast them again. The place was quiet, so peaceful and safe that I could hardly believe that it had almost ended our lives.

We cut some more firewood to keep the fire going and warm the refuge up. Besides, we had to cut enough wood so as to leave more than we had found there. You must never forget the rule of the hiker, to show gratitude towards people, towards the refuge that shelters you and brings you comfort, towards that oasis amidst a desert of endless isolation.

It was suddenly night time, before we even realized. Leo used the sat phone to talk to Hernán, who was in charge of sending a vehicle to pick us up at the end of our trip. Leo told him that we would be in Estancia María Luisa in about four days. Giving up, I took my lines out of the river. I said to myself, once again, that fishing was not my thing. But I would give it another shot, whenever I had the chance. I would never give up.

We had lentils with rice for dinner, but this time we added grated cheese. That was indeed a luxury. We talked about many things until about two in the morning, by the faint and warm light of the fire.

Before going to bed, I went outside for a while. The sky, like that time at Puerto Español, was filled with stars. The night was deep blue, even more blue than the ocean itself; the stars were as white as snow flakes, but a lot brighter, like watery eyes that are about to create a tear. I am very grateful for having lived moments like those. When I saw something like that, I immediately forgot about all the negative things. I buried bad memories deep in my mind. I cared more about the positive things in life - they were more important to me. Sadness would simply vanish.

DAY 33 For the second time on our whole expedition, we decided to take shifts to keep the fire alive. My shift was from four to half past five in the morning. I slept another hour after that, and Leo woke us up at seven with breakfast. We drank coffee with milk and ate *tortas fritas*. That was grand. After such a tasty meal, we started organizing everything. Juan and I cut more firewood to leave more than we had found. We cleaned everything up and we bade Bueno River goodbye. After all, the place brought us as many bitter as happy memories. We could say that we struck a balance there.

It was half past ten when we left and started walking along Mesa de Orozco, named that by Elizalde. At noon we got to Noguera or Leticia River. It was a déjà vu, because we had the same feeling as when we got to Bueno River. We were on a hill and from there we saw the course that the river ran, it was very similar to that of Bueno River. There was also a bridge very similar to the previous one, and, ironically enough, it went only half way across. We went down to the shore, and Leo looked for a crossing point. After a couple of attempts, he found one. The water level was alright, but the flow was so fast that I knew that should I slip, I would end up floating in the ocean. We managed to cross successfully and we were in a good mood to keep going.

We kept up a fast pace; it was a beautiful day and we felt like walking. We had been lucky with the weather once again; the sky was clear, not a single cloud in sight.

At Leticia Cape, we found an old run-down refuge, which seemed to be on the verge of collapsing. Outside there were tables, chairs and other pieces of furniture that had once been used by the adventurers who had lived here. Near the ocean, we found several young kelp geese, a typical bird in Tierra del Fuego.

We left the beach and went up the hill. We stopped there to eat and drink something hot. It was not good to stop for long; when our bodies wanted warmth, the cold was even more intense. So we continued walking, trying to get to our destination. We stopped at half past five. We decided to set up the tent on top of a small hill. The spot was far from ideal, for there was no firewood and no streams nearby, so we had to use water from the peat bog, which looked rather darkish. To compensate, it offered a marvellous view. The sun was setting, seemingly going into the ocean, which reflected its last rays; the day was coming to an end.

While Leo and Juan set up the tent, I looked for the water we needed for that night and the next morning. We organized everything, we put our things inside, we changed clothes and we drank some hot tea. Later on I took a nap for about two hours. Juan woke me up when the food was ready. We had dinner and as soon as we finished I went to bed. We were very tired; we had slept only three hours the previous night.

DAY 34 We had run out of supplies for a complete breakfast a long time ago; cereals, dry fruit, nuts, hazelnuts; the 'product mix' as we had called it. As of late, our mornings were more in the old traditions of our country: *mate* and *tortas fritas*. I was the first one to exit the tent. The reward was to get to see those idyllic shades of pink, orange and yellow, besides getting to see about ten condors in that amazing sky. We were near the end, but nature kept on giving us wonderful gifts day after day.

The trail was clearly marked, as if an imaginary painter had painted it there just for us, for us to follow it all the way, for us to get to our final destination. We were taking it easy, keeping the rhythm set by the song that we sang that sunny morning. We went down to the beach; the tide was low, so we could walk easily on the firm sand, enjoying the absence of obstacles. After walking on that highway-like beach for a long time, we got to a hill marked by some posts. It was high and steep, and the ground was a kind of clay that gave way when we stepped on it. Aided by my walking poles and grabbing some posts, I managed to get to the top. We found a fence and a sign that said that we were still inside Estancia Policarpo, in La Chaira department. We went past the sign and, at a distance, we saw some houses. We heard about ten dogs starting to bark and then a shout from someone who was there obviously wondering what was upsetting the dogs. There was more than one building there; there was a big house and some other smaller houses, surely a meat deposit, a tool shack, bathroom and spice room. The farmer invited us into his house. He introduced himself as Ainol. It was about noon; perhaps we would have made it to Estancia María Luisa if we had set ourselves to it, but we agreed to stay there, learning the ways of the local farmer, getting to know his story and secrets of his world, enjoying the ever-present hospitality that characterizes Argentinean *gauchos*.

Ainol had no problems with letting us spend the night there; in fact, he fixed us lunch, some *tortas fritas* for tea and barbecue for dinner. Of course we drank some *mate*, and we talked long after the sun had set, by the light of a moon that eventually dipped into the ocean until the next day. As with other farmers that we met in the course of our adventure, talking to Ainol was a way of learning more about the habits and beliefs of the country people, about their myths, about their lifestyle, so different to ours, which sometimes showed a degree of introspection, a departure from the shallowness and consumerism that prevail in our modern society. It was interesting to discover a common characteristic to Ainol, Pati and Correntino in the way they spoke, how they put their ideas into words, and their vision of life. It is true that there are not many true *gauchos* left, but those who live on are more alive than ever.

At night, while drinking a good cup of tea by the faint light of a kerosene lamp, I wrote an entry in my diary and recorded the hours that we had walked every day so far. I remember that I looked at our worn out black and white satellite image, and I had a hard time believing that we were about to accomplish our goal - just one last river, one last beach, one last and unforgettable day, the final day of the 'Nomads in Mitre'.

DAY 35 Early in the morning, we heard sounds coming from the main room of the house. We noticed that Ainol was lighting the fire, heating up some water and getting ready to drink some *mate*. Then, silence; surely waiting for the water to heat up. We hurried and got up; we did not want to miss that magical moment that you find only early in the morning when you are away from the city. The morning went by quickly; before we realized it, it was already noon. Ainol was fixing lunch, but we had to leave; the tide was waning and we still had to cross Yrigoyen River. As a token of our appreciation for the hospitality that we received at La Chaira outpost, Leo gave Ainol a t-shirt. After repacking our bags, we headed out to finish off the adventure we had started thirty five days ago, on a sunny autumn morning.

And speaking about sunny mornings, this one was as sunny as it can get. It was cold, but the sun shone everywhere; once again it bathed us, giving us its warm embrace and shining for our delight. After two hours, we got to Yrigoyen River. We crossed it near the shoreline and with the water up to our knees; it was quite fast-flowing, but we had no major problems. We celebrated briefly after having crossed our last obstacle, the river that was the border of the territory called the Mitre Peninsula, of those lands I had dreamt about so many times and which I was leaving behind having walked through them, having experienced them so intensely.

We were already relaxed; we were only a few hours away from our final destination. The situation and the beauty of that day made it perfect for pictures, so I shot the sky, the beach, the ocean that would be part of my permanent memories. I guess that I thought I would not settle for the images that I had stored in my brain. I needed to have concrete evidence; I would have never forgiven myself for not being able to share that wonderful place with my loved ones upon my return. It was all too perfect to keep it to myself.

We continued moving forward along the beach line until we got to a trail that led to a fishing lodge. In the summer, fishermen go there because of the quantity and quality of fish that are usually caught. Trout caught there are usually about four to five kilos. We kept moving until the trail became a road. We had done it; we were moving at ease now, kind of like cars with no engines, no noise, no polluting fumes; we had no horns, mirrors, steering wheels, but we did have a course, a place where we were going, a final destination: Estancia María Luisa.

We got there a few hours later, at about five in the afternoon. Leo was walking a little ahead of us when he found a fence. He opened it. He waved to us with his walking poles, meaning that was it, that we had reached the end; that thirty-five days of walking ended right there; that they would come and get us with a vehicle and that we would no longer be forced to use our weary legs to move from one place to another; that we would not have to be nomads anymore; that we would go back to town and, thus, go back to a sedentary life; that the only thing that would remain alive about this would be the sweet memories, the experiences of three men, three fortunes that had been one for a month, a small team that, actually, was way more than large. The awareness of our strengths and weaknesses, of the hopes that motivate souls, of souls that motivate bodies, and bodies that are worthless without the other two to push them; the awareness that when we thought we could not go on any further, we always could, that when our legs were too tired to go on, we walked with our minds; above all things, the awareness that there are no such things as supermen, but super wills.

7
MissionAccomplished

Arrival of the 'Nomads' at Estancia María Luisa

To us, opening the gate at Estancia María Luisa meant something more than leaving one territory and entering another. That ordinary, everyday act of pushing the wooden gate open had a coded meaning that I was not prepared to decipher. Or maybe I was, but I did not intend to.

Before introducing ourselves to the person in charge of the estancia, we started preparing for the celebrations that an event of this magnitude called for. Of course, it was a very emotional moment, full of embraces, laughs and tears. And we even played a small spoof speculating on the welcome that was awaiting us.

As usual, the reception by the ranch foreman was exceptional. Mr. Vera welcomed us in an amicable and generous tone. He promptly accommodated us in a cabin that had more amenities than we could have hoped for. For us a simple roof over our heads would do, but that little wooden house was equipped with a stove, which we lit up as soon as we got there, beds and even a bathroom. Mr. Vera left us alone to let us make ourselves at home, and we seized on the opportunity to drink some warm *mate*. Later, this good man came back to tell us that dinner was ready. Such a generous offer did not surprise us at all because, during the expedition, I learnt that rural people not only offer travellers everything they have at hand, but also go out of their way to be helpful. It is amazing to find these extraordinary characters helping strangers they know absolutely nothing about. It is not only surprising, but also deeply gratifying to encounter these people, whose souls display noble values such as a kindness and generosity that make them transcend ordinary life.

Without delay, we accepted the kind invitation and followed Mr. Vera into his house. Isabel, a short, friendly lady, introduced herself as Mr. Vera's wife and housekeeper. I was impressed by how impeccable it all was. The prevailing cleanliness showed in every inch of that residence, which was brimming with love and care. Each little detail was a bright touch that gave the whole room a family warmth and made you feel at home. The salamander was the perfect example of how immaculate it all looked, for even though it was heating the room, there was not a single wood chip in sight that could give away the fire in its iron belly.

Isabel treated us to roasted lamb with potatoes, and it all tasted homemade, with that special flavor mothers put in their cooking. As a token of our appreciation, we gave the kind woman our last chocolate bar. When coffee arrived, we shared some footage of our long expedition that we had captured with our camera. They both seemed to enjoy the movie show that we put on for a few minutes.

Mr. Vera and Isabel's story is like the story of many other couples that decide to work in rural areas. In fact, we could draw a comparison between them and the first couple we encountered - Juan Carlos and Ramona - whom we had met many kilometres ago on the shores of Beagle Channel, at the historic Estancia Harberton. Like them, Mr. Vera and Isabel, born in Chile, had worked in different estancias of the province: Mr. Vera as a foreman and Isabel as the housekeeper of the main house. Hundreds of kilometres separated one couple from the other, but they share similar values. The human factor is at the core of their being and transcends everything; it is what makes them so special.

We thanked them for the warm treatment and we went to bed, saying we would see them again for breakfast the next morning.

Before going to our bedroom, we visited Germán and Ezequiel, two of the farm workers. We spent a long while with them, drinking *mates* and chatting about different topics. They were curious about our journey and we gladly provided details of many of the best and worst moments. They told us about their jobs, which were not connected with sheep, but with the ranch sawmill. I turned in earlier than Leo and Juan, because I was feeling really tired and needed some rest.

DAY 36 I THE FINAL DAY

We got up at around 8:30 a.m. Leo was in charge of heating the stove and preparing some *mates* to start the day. Two hours later, we were at Mr. Vera's, ready to enjoy the anticipated country breakfast. The homemade bread was delicious and, combined with butter, marmalade and hot coffee, was something to be praised. When we ran out of butter, we wanted to ask for more but no one dared bother Isabel.

As none of us volunteered, we tossed for it and I lost, which left me in charge of the task, while Leo and Juan laughed. After the morning feast, it was shower time. One by one, we went into that hot water confessional where we would be cleansed, leaving behind all the traces of dirt, sand, mud and wood that we were carrying. Our nomad spirit was condemned to stay there, to live in exile, in the solitude of the Mitre Peninsula, just where it had been born and had thrived. Those essences that had accompanied us for so long, and which our noses had grown so fond of, were to disappear under clean steamy water, and we emerged from that cleansing ceremony with a different countenance from that we had displayed for over a month - we were finally re-entering civilization.

Before we left the house to organize our gear for departure, Isabel urged us not to go too far, since she would be waiting for us with lunch. We would certainly stick around - we didn't want to make her, or her food, wait for us. We could not turn down such a lovely invitation, especially since we knew that the cook was excellent.

By noon, everything was ready for departure, and after an unforgettable lunch, we visited the sawmill facilities with Ezequiel and Germán. The day was favourable in every way. The air was peaceful and the sunbeams filtered though the gaps between the leaves of hundreds of *lengas* that seemed to reach up to the sky; the wind gently caressed the tree tops, as a father pushing his child in the swings, and the tree crowns answered with a velvety whisper, as soft as a lullaby.

The only thing that disturbed the tranquility was the green monster of a truck that took us along the track to the sawmill.

Juan Manuel Ronco drinking *mate* during one of our stops.

It's huge wheels churned the mud, while the powerful engine roared in protest. The trip to the sawmill was exihilirating, and we laughed and shouted with happiness.

Our guides gave us a short but informative talk about how the sawmill worked as they showed us the machinery and pointed out the methods and processes involved in forestry work.

After the visit, we went back to the main house in the estancia. When we were near the house, we saw a four-by-four from a distance, and we realized that it was our means of transport back into the city. Our assumption was confirmed when we saw our friends celebrating, as we approached the house. One of Juan's workmates and friends, Beto, came to welcome us, followed by a small delegation comprising his wife and our friend Lucas Ramos. It could be said that the reunion with them was my first contact with civilization. After the embraces and the warm welcome of the 'Nomads' by our reception party, each of us started to ask about the most important news of the past 36 days. On the one hand, I wanted to find out about the events of the past month and to see my family and closest friends, but on the other hand, I wanted to remain in that world where the very essence and meaning of life had meant so much. I knew that was impossible, because coming back to the city would mean reintegrating to society, which entailed going back to work, paying the rent, complying with schedules and following rules and routines in order to fit in the framework of the system.

Without much delay, we started loading our baggage into the four-by-four in order to embark on the final stage of our return journey back home. As we said our goodbyes, we took a few minutes to thank Mr. Vera and Isabel from the bottom of our hearts for all they had done for us, and the good woman surprised us once again with an invitation that no one could refuse: a country afternoon feast. For the occasion, the wonderful lady delighted us with a plentiful tray of *tortas fritas*, homemade bread, butter and *dulce de leche*. We would never have forgiven ourselves if we had missed such good coffee with those sweet treats. Once again, the values of the country people became imprinted in my heart forever.

We were now ready to leave. We said our final goodbyes to everyone in the estancia, and set our for home along Provincial Route A, a winding gravel road, as the day started to take on soft pink, yellowish and dark tones. Finally, all was black and the heavy darkness of the night started to transform objects into featureless silhouettes, shapeless shadows and blurry ghosts.

The journey back was made more enjoyable by an interesting conversation we had with Beto about living on an island and the implications for its inhabitants. After the discussion, I spent most of the journey in introspection, thinking deeply about the feelings in my heart, but still trying to objectively analyze everything Mitre had meant to me. I concluded that the trip had been much more than a dream come true; it also meant a unique way of isolating us from all the earthly possessions and finding the essence of things, learning to value what is important in life, realizing how superfluous material possessions are, discovering our true selves, without masks or armour, and understanding the world with the perceptions of our hearts and souls.

Going deep into the core of the Mitre Peninsula had made me more aware of two opposite, different planes of reality. The first one had to do with everyday life in the city, with society and its cyclic routine; I realized that, in the long term, this reality led to mediocrity, to conformism, to the numbness of habit and the subsequent loss of the ability to be astonished and surprised. The second aspect was related to the possibility of having a full life, a new world where every day brought new discoveries, a life full of hope, truth and also fear. This was a reality that, no doubt, led to union, friendship and teamwork towards a common goal. This reality, in its broad sense, meant only one thing: illumination. Speaking of which, I have to say that our arrival in the small town of Tolhuin (by National Route 3, on the way to Ushuaia) just in the center of the island, was somewhat illuminating - and bewildering because we magically came face to face with hundreds of little lights that gave their glow to the night. But these were electric bulbs and not the big bonfires I had grown accustomed to on the inhospitable and deserted coasts of Tierra del Fuego. We made a stop at a bakery called La Unión to buy something to eat. When I reached for my wallet to pay, it was a funny surprise to find it full of moss. That green presence was not a consequence of lack of use, but because it had got wet when we crossed the cold waters of Bompland River. I should have dried it before putting it away, but as you can imagine, I did not.

The last hundred kilometres that separated Tolhuin from Ushuaia felt like a final countdown before we arrived home. On the way in, I realized that I would miss the solitude in Mitre. But still, I was glad to be back in my town and with my people. Being away from everything had made me love more deeply everything that I had previously taken for granted, including my family and friends.

It was a very intense feeling to finally be back home, in Ushuaia, the southernmost city in the world. I felt an outsider in that moment, as if I was not in the vehicle that drove along streets full of cars and people. It was like coming from another time, from a place where we had grown accustomed to do without, from another dimension. Being in the city again made me feel that I was recovering something, a life I had abandoned 36 days ago. But it was not the night smells or the urban noises or the familiar houses that really made me feel that I was coming back to my place. What really made me feel at home again was none of that, but something much simpler; something as simple and moving as the high-pitched voice of a child, a boy calling his father. As soon as Beto stopped the four-by-four at Leo's door, one of his children cried out loudly 'Dad!' Right in that instant, I felt joy overcome me, because it dawned on me that we had returned home.

8
Epilogue

My first expedition to the Mitre Peninsula enriched me enormously. Once we had completed the adventure, we used our photographs and all the knowledge acquired to give dozens of talks in different schools of Ushuaia during the winter months. Our goal was to share our experience so as to raise awareness among young kids about the importance of love and care for nature. We would speak at length about topics such as flora, fauna, ecology and history. To make the lectures more interesting, we would project slides, highlighting the most important points or show pictures that depicted the key moments in our expedition. I remember that the young students would listen, astonished, to the stories of these three madmen who had walked along hundreds of kilometres on the very same island that they inhabited. They showed great interest and asked questions, which, in many cases, surprised us because of how complex and deep they were. We were more than happy to answer each of these questions from the curious students. Each picture we showed of each mysterious place visited, of each dawn and dusk evoked memories that we shared with the young listeners, and made my mind return to my special peninsula. I felt that I missed those wild landscapes more and more, especially those cliffs that touched the ocean waters and the infinite sky.

I dreamt of those long days when we would march for hours on end along deserted beaches, accompanied solely by the song of the sea and the sound of our own steps in the sand. I do not know if it was a whim or mere chance or an incredible random alignment of the planets, but the truth is that almost without realizing what I was doing, eleven months after my first expedition to the Mitre Peninsula, I found myself going back to the place that had given me so much. The expedition 'Back to Mitre' was a reality. It was obvious that the peninsula had cast a spell on me, an irresistible attraction that seduced my soul, my mind and my senses. An attraction that compelled me to go back to those lands, to continue searching for the ghost, the nomadic spirit that was surely still haunting those parts. There was a kind of magnetism, an invisible bond that was supernaturally powerful and which lured me into seeking out again the source of this strange spell. My fellow travellers would be different ones; this time I would share the adventure with Carlos Signoni (37) and Raúl Ranzani (42), both nature enthusiasts and outdoors lovers. The route would be the same, but instead of having Ushuaia as our starting point, we would set out from Estancia Moat. The trails and paths would be similar to the previous journey, but there was a new world ahead to be discovered, a world that had nothing to do with the landscape or the road, but with the intricate twists and turns of human relations. Once again, we would live hundreds of adventures and misadventures at the ends of the earth. But all of that is, dear reader, part of another story...

Acknowledgements

I would like to express my gratitude to the following people and organizations: to Leo and Juan, who helped me exploring the beautiful area of the Mitre Peninsula, and for borrowing me some excellent pictures that I use in this book, to Don Taylor, who helped me a lot in the hard task of correcting and polishing the pages of *Fire Walking*, to Adolfo Imbert, Beto Brizuela, Sergio Anselmino, Carlos Signoni and Raúl Ranzani, to Osvaldo Bianchi, Carlos from Chocolatería Ushuaia, to Juan Domingo Vázquez, to Librería Rayuela, to everyone at the Museo del Fin del Mundo, to Banco de Tierra del Fuego, to Foto Eduardo, to Juan Pablo Ortiz, Felipe Lobert, to Mr. Moreno Preto and Catamaranes Canoero, to María Angélica from All Patagonia, to the Argentinean Navy, especially to the staff in outpost A. R. A. Buen Suceso Bay, to Makalu, Pati and Correntino, to Juan Carlos and Ramona from Estancia Harberton, to Nelson Ainol and Mr. Oyarsún from La Chaira outpost, to Mr. Vera and Isabel from Estancia María Luisa, to Hernán, Esteban, Gustavo and Beto from Canal Fun, to Lucas Ramos, Mariano Melidone, Mr. Alejandro Suárez Molina, María Laura Borla, Tomás Gerhardt, and all the schools that received us for the talks on the 'Nomads in Mitre' Expedition for all their warmth, and, of course, to all our friends and family members, who were part of the before, the during and the after of this expedition.

F. E. G.
Ushuaia, July 2007

Bibliography

CANCLINI, Arnoldo, *Hasta lo último de la tierra,* La Aurora, Buenos Aires, 1978.

CANCLINI, Arnoldo (director), *Ushuaia, 1884-1984. Cien años de una ciudad argentina,* Ushuaia, Municipalidad de Ushuaia, 1984.

BELZA, Juan E., *Romancero del Topónimo Fueguino: discusión histórica desde su origen y fortuna,* Buenos Aires, Publicación del Instituto de Investigaciones Históricas de Tierra del Fuego, 1978.

BRIDGES, Lucas, *El último confín de la tierra (The Uttermost Part of the Earth),* Marymar Ediciones, Buenos Aires, 1978.

CARRARA, Ítalo Santiago, *Lobos marinos, pingüinos y guaneras de las costas del litoral marítimo e islas adyacentes de la República Argentina,* La Plata, Universidad de la Plata, Facultad de Ciencias Veterinarias, 1952.

EL FUEGUINO, *'Naufragio en el Beagle',* Newspaper article, Ushuaia, 22 de enero de 1988.

GUSINDE, Martín, *Los Indios de Tierra del Fuego,* Tomo II, Buenos Aires, Centro Argentino de Etnología Americana, Consejo Nacional de Investigaciones Científicas y Técnicas, 1986.

INSTITUTO DE INVESTIGACIONES HISTÓRICAS DE TIERRA DEL FUEGO, *Karukinka,* Cuaderno Fueguino Nº3, Buenos Aires, 1973.

INSTITUTO GEOGRÁFICO MILITAR, *Toponimia de la República Argentina, Territorio Nacional de Tierra del Fuego,* Buenos Aires, 1982.

LISTA, Ramón, *Obras,* Tomo II, Buenos Aires, Editorial Confluencia, 1998.

OSTOICH, Pedro and Arnoldo CANCLINI (col.), *Un Solitario en Tierra del Fuego,* Ushuaia, Zagier & Urruty, 2000.

POPPER, Julio, *Atlanta. Proyecto para la fundación de un pueblo marítimo en Tierra del Fuego y otros escritos,* Buenos Aires, Eudeba, 2003.

SUBSECRETARÍA DE PLANEAMIENTO DE LA CIUDAD DE USHUAIA, *Península Mitre. Proyecto de creación de un área protegida en el extremo sudoriental de la Isla Grande de Tierra del Fuego, República Argentina,* Ushuaia, 2002.

ZANOLA, Pablo Oscar, *'Otro fantasma en la navegación austral',* article published in PEOAF 84 (Programa del Extremo Oriental del Archipiélago Fueguino), Museo del Fin del Mundo, Ushuaia, 1986.